Hezekiah Butterworth

Stories from China

Hezekiah Butterworth

Stories from China

ISBN/EAN: 9783337004347

Printed in Europe, USA, Canada, Australia, Japan

Cover: Foto ©ninafisch / pixelio.de

More available books at **www.hansebooks.com**

STORIES FROM CHINA

BY THE

AUTHOR OF "THE STORY OF A SUMMER DAY"
"TRAVELLERS' TALES," ETC.

WITH TWENTY-FIVE ILLUSTRATIONS

SEELEY, JACKSON, AND HALLIDAY, 54, FLEET STREET
LONDON. MDCCCLXXVI.

CONTENTS.

	PAGE
CHAPTER I.	
EXAMINATIONS	1
CHAPTER II.	
GROPINGS IN THE DARK	6
CHAPTER III.	
SOME CHINESE WONDERS	27
CHAPTER IV.	
GIRLS AND WOMEN	46
CHAPTER V.	
WRETCHEDNESS	66
CHAPTER VI.	
OPIUM AND TEA	84
CHAPTER VII.	
PEKIN, NANKIN, AND CANTON	107
CHAPTER VIII.	
UNDAUNTED BY DIFFICULTIES	132

CONTENTS.

CHAPTER IX.
Hang-chow 155

CHAPTER X.
Hongkong and the Taepings 177

CHAPTER XI.
Soldiers 202

STORIES FROM CHINA.

CHAPTER I.

EXAMINATIONS.

"HURRAH! hurrah! Jem's in. The telegram has come. 'Passed 10th.' Isn't it splendid?" Thus exclaimed Tom Foster, as he rushed one day into his sisters' schoolroom, where two little girls were quietly engaged in preparing their lessons. Down went the books, and away rushed Mabel and Grace to see the precious paper, and rejoice with their widowed mother in the good news which it had brought. Most anxiously that yellow document had been looked for for some days, and very painful had been the last few weeks of suspense, for it was of the utmost importance that Jem should succeed. Mrs. Foster's means were very limited, and she had pinched herself and her younger children in every possible way, in order that her elder son should go up to the Civil Service examination well prepared.

The rejoicing, therefore, over that telegram can well be imagined, and after every letter almost had been carefully examined, Mabel declared that it was too precious to be destroyed, and begged it of her mother that she might put it away carefully in her box of treasures.

"When will such happy tidings come of you, Tom?" said Mrs. Foster, as she gave the paper to the little girl.

"Oh never," replied Tom. "I shall never go in for an examination. I hate them too much; even those we have at school, and a thing like this must be far worse."

"How do you propose to get into the Royal Engineers then," said his mother, "as you often say you mean to do? Have you some powerful friend who has promised you an appointment regardless of your merits?"

Tom laughed. "Oh, I don't know, mother," he said. "I suppose I must be something else, a doctor, or a lawyer or something."

"But even for a doctor or a lawyer you would have to make up your mind for examinations," replied

Mrs. Foster. "They are the fashion of the day, and unless you resolve to go into trade, I am afraid you can't avoid them."

Tom looked sober. "It is very horrid," he said; "I wish we lived in some other country."

"Perhaps you would like to be a South Sea Islander," said Mabel; "one of those fine fellows that we heard about the other day, who think themselves handsomely dressed in a pair of top-boots and a necklace. I should not think you would be bothered with competitive examinations there. And if the style of living is as simple as that of dress, it cannot be important to have a large income."

"Of course I don't want to be a savage," replied Tom. "I should like to be a Chinese or a Japanese. They were civilized ages before we were—weren't they, mother?"

"Certainly Tom," said Mrs. Foster, "and had competitive examinations too, ages before we thought of them. I am afraid you would not escape them by going to China. Do not you know that promotion of every kind is decided by examinations in China?"

"Is it really, mother?" exclaimed Tom. "Do you mean that the fellows with pigtails have to answer troublesome questions like Jem?"

"Certainly, and write essays too, only on far more uninteresting subjects than those which are given in England. Indeed the examinations in China, instead of helping on the progress of the nation, rather tend to check it, for everything like originality is discouraged, and the test of excellence consists in a close resemblance, both in sentiment and style, with the writings of the ancient philosophers. But the anxiety of the candidates to pass is just as great as among ourselves, and there is much the same excitement among the friends. Each examination successfully got through, confers a certain degree upon the happy individual, and so great is the enthusiasm for literary distinction, that instances have been known of men persevering even to their seventieth or eightieth year, in their attempts to obtain some of the higher degrees."

"What silly old fellows!" said Tom. "But I had not the least idea that the Chinese were people of that kind. I did not know that they cared about books."

"I don't suppose you know much about them at all," said Grace. "I am sure I don't. I know the people wear pigtails, and are a great deal too fond of opium, and that tea comes from China, and that the Emperor of China does not like foreigners, but that is about all. I wish I did know more about them. Oh, mamma," she continued quickly, "I have thought of such a capital idea. You know you have just finished the book that you were reading to us at our 'Children's Working Party,' and you said you did not know what to read next. I wish, instead of reading any book at all, you would just tell us interesting stories about China. It would be so much nicer."

"A very fine idea, indeed," said Mrs. Foster; "but pray where am I to find the stories."

"Oh, mamma," exclaimed both the girls, "I am sure you could, and it would be so much nicer than a book. Do say you will. The girls would like it so much better, and then perhaps some more boys would come. Fred Johnson said the other day that he did so like to listen to your stories, and he can make such pretty frames, and he illuminates so well. I am sure his things would sell well. Do promise to try, there is a dear good mother."

"Nothing like a little coaxing and flattering, you think?" said Mrs. Foster smiling. "Well, if you really wish it, I will see if I can find anything interesting to tell you at the next working party, and if my stories should prove very dull and uninteresting, we will have a book the time after."

CHAPTER II.

GROPINGS IN THE DARK.

ABOUT a week after the conversation just related, a large party of children assembled at The Bingle. Mabel and Grace had been very energetic in their endeavours to induce some boys to join their monthly missionary working party, and by the promise that they should have a table all to themselves, and, as one of them expressed it, "should be in no way mixed up with needles and cotton," had succeeded in persuading four or five to attend. Fred Johnson was there, with his colour-box and cardboard; Frank Mason, who was first rate at making ships and boats of all descriptions; John Stoker, whose cardboard models were the wonder and admiration of all his young friends; and one or two others, whose talents as yet were undeveloped. At first Tom had declared that nothing would induce him to be present, that working parties were only fit for girls, but when he found that some of his special friends had really consented to accept Mabel's invitation, he managed to pocket his boyish dignity and importance, and take his place with the rest.

When all were seated, and all the little preliminary arrangements of the work were completed, Mrs. Foster began :—

"I mean to tell you to-day a little about the religion of China—or, rather, the religions, for there are three—that of Confucius, that of the Taouists, and Buddhism. When you have heard a little about each, you will see how much the poor Chinese need our help, and how utterly incapable even the most civilized people are to find out God and the way of salvation when left unaided. I will tell you first about Confucianism, because that is the religion of the educated classes. Confucius was a wise man who lived about the time of Daniel, and compiled what are called the Canonical Books of History. Some of these books appear to be very ancient indeed—in fact to have been written not long after the time of Noah; and they contain a great deal that is very wise and beautiful. Some of the sentences resemble verses in the Proverbs or Psalms, and probably were first of all spoken by holy men of old while yet a knowledge of the true God lingered in the earth. They speak of one Supreme Being as Creator and Preserver, and attribute to him the attributes of omniscience and omnipresence.

"Certain men attached themselves to Confucius, and became his disciples, following him about from place to place, and listening to his teaching. To these men Confucius continually quoted from the old books, and urged their study, but, at the same time, sad to say, his teaching tended rather to dim than to brighten the poor Chinese's knowledge of God, and to discourage their efforts 'to feel after Him, if haply they might find Him.' He directed the attention of his followers far more to the morality than to the religion contained in the books. He abandoned the use of the name of God, and generally employed the vaguer one of Heaven. He spoke little of the love and gratitude which we owe to our Heavenly Father for all the blessings which He pours down upon us, and though he continually urged the people to the practice of virtue, he gave them no motive strong enough to make them follow his counsels. In the old books there is a distinct reference to the fall: 'Man no longer has what he had before the fall, and he has brought his children into his misery. O Heaven! you only can help us. Wipe away the stains of the father, and save his children,' is a sentence that may be found in them. But Confucius taught that 'man's nature is good;' and he not only thought it possible to attain perfection, but believed that it had been attained by many sages of antiquity."

"Did he think he was perfect himself, mamma?" inquired Tom. "I never can understand any one doing that."

"No, though he thought it attainable, he confessed that he had not attained it."

"What did he think became of people after death?" inquired Mabel. "Did he believe in heaven and hell?"

"He confessed himself perfectly ignorant. All his teaching was confined to the duties of this world. 'I do not understand life,' he said, 'how can I know death?' But he does not seem to have imagined that there is any hereafter for the soul. 'You die, and it is all over with you,' is one of his sayings. The only immortality in which he believed was the immortality of fame, an immortality which would do little to comfort or support any one when on a dying bed. So you see that as far as the Confucianists are concerned there is sad need of missionaries in China."

"But, I suppose, Mrs. Foster," inquired one of the children, "if the Confucianists do not think much about God at all, they at any rate do not worship idols?"

"Not exactly," replied Mrs. Foster. "Indeed they profess a profound contempt for idolatry; but at the same time, in all the great cities of the empire, temples are built in memory of the great sage, and, unwilling as he might have been to receive such honour, his memorial tablet is worshipped as if it were a god."

"What do you mean by his memorial tablet, mamma?" inquired Grace. "I do not understand. Is it something like the tablets that are put up in our churches when people die."

"Not very different," replied Mrs. Foster. "All the Chinese, I must tell you, whether Confucianists, Buddhists, or Taouists, have an immense reverence for the memory of their ancestors. In fact, though it may have been only reverence in the first instance, the feeling soon became more than that, and, though images of Confucius are very seldom seen, the worship of his tablet, and, in fact, that of all ancestral tablets, is just as truly idolatrous as if the people bowed down before the most hideous image that was ever made!"

"But what makes them worship the tablets?" inquired one of the children. "It seems such a funny thing to do."

"They imagine that the tablet is the departed spirit's throne, or rather the throne of one of the souls. For they believe every one to have three souls, one of which is laid in the grave with the body, another goes to judgment, and the third mounts into the tablet. The tablet is placed either in some recess in the house or in the ancestral temple, and before it are offered, from time to time, the food and clothing and money which the dead man is thought to need in the other world."

"But, mamma," said Mabel, "you said just now that Confucius confessed himself quite ignorant of what happened to people when they died, and seemed to believe only in the immortality of fame."

"True, and yet it was he who first taught the people to worship the departed. Perhaps at first the worship was merely an exaggerated way of reverencing their memory; but the people in general were not likely to be satisfied with such very vague ideas of the unseen world as those put forth by Confucius, and, accordingly, the popular superstitions are much more explicit. The general belief is that the unseen world is an exact counterpart of this, only that everything is spiritualized. The departed spirits are supposed to need food, clothes, and money, just as much as they did when they lived in bodies, and it is the duty of their living friends to provide them with these. In order to make them fit for the spirits' use, however, they have to be burnt, and as no unfortunate Chinese could afford to supply all his departed ancestors with real clothes and money, they make them of paper. The food which is offered before the ancestral tablets is real, but then that is not wasted, for after it has steamed away for some little time, the spirits are said to have consumed all the spiritual part, and the survivors feast on the remains. Besides the regular worship of dead relatives, periodical feasts are given to the beggar ghosts. These beggar ghosts are the spirits of those who have died, and for some reason have remained unburied, such as those who have been drowned, or have been slain in battle. These poor unfortunate spirits are thought to wander about in a state of utter misery, homeless, and unfed. They are supposed to be exceedingly troublesome and annoying if left uncared for, and, therefore, in self-defence, those who dread their power from time to time supply their wants. It is calculated that thirty millions sterling is every year spent upon these imaginary beggars."

"What an enormous sum!" exclaimed Tom; "but I suppose it is not all wasted, for I suppose somebody eats the food which is provided for the ghosts."

"Certainly!" replied his mother. "After a number of prayers have been said by the priests, and certain forms have been gone through, a signal is given and there is a general scramble for the spoil. A missionary gives an account of one of these festivals, at which he says nearly two thousand persons were present; but all the food—and it was provided on a most liberal scale—disappeared in an instant. No doubt the real living beggars are not sorry when the day for the ghost beggars' festival comes round; for though the food which the spirits leave is said to have lost all its nourishing qualities, the people who eat it probably find it tastes very good."

"It seems such a queer idea to worship your dead grandfathers and great-grandfathers!" said one of the boys, "I cannot think whatever made Confucius or any one else think of such a thing. But the Chinese always treat their parents with great respect when they are alive, don't they?"

"Yes," replied Mrs. Foster. "No nation, I should think, has ever so thoroughly obeyed the fifth commandment as the Chinese, and you see the promise has come true—they have dwelt long in the land.

"But I must tell you now a little about Buddhism. It was not introduced into China until 700 years after the time of Confucius, and had its origin in India. Gautama Buddha was the founder of the sect, and he is the chief object which is held up before the people by the priests for their worship and imitation. All the gods, in fact, occupy a position subordinate to him— a man self-purified and exalted. Buddhism is, in fact, the worship of the perfect man, and the hightest state of happiness which its devotees aspire to reach is termed the Nirwana. This is a state when, by self-mortification and reflection, sin and evil are completely overcome, and the soul, being no longer excited by either pleasure or pain, sinks into a kind of nothingness, and, if it does not cease to exist, becomes at any rate unconscious of its existence. But this state of supposed bliss, the bare idea of which is to me utterly horrible, is only attained by a few of those who are thought very great saints. The majority of ordinary mortals pass from body to body of animals or men— now upwards, it may be, in the scale of being, and now downwards, according as they are good or bad. If a poor man, for instance, lives a good life, he hopes next time to be born a rich man, and then, perhaps, a prince, and so on until at last he attains the Nirwana. But, if he is wicked, he is told that his spirit will go into some loathsome beast or reptile. This idea of the transmigration of souls causes the stricter Buddhists to abstain from animal food, as they never feel quite sure that the spirits of some relation may not inhabit the animals they would need to kill.

"But, besides this system of rewards and punishments, the Buddhists believe in a purgatory—for those, I suppose, who have been too wicked to be allowed any body again of any kind. The priests, or Bonzes, as they are called, make a great deal of money out of this purgatory. If any of the priests make the acquaintance of a rich Chinaman, they are pretty sure to discover in a short time that the soul of some relative is suffering in this place of torment. They take care that a rich man shall be informed of the fact, and when consulted by the latter, as is generally the case, they recommend a long and expensive ceremonial as the surest means of relieving the poor tormented spirit. When asked the cost, they name a large sum, at which the man is pretty sure to haggle. The contest generally goes on for a little time, and then, when the priest finds his victim will not yield, he offers to try what he can do for a smaller sum. The ceremonies begin, and there is a great beating of gongs and burning of incense; but in a little while the priest is almost sure to stop his incantations, and with a look of the greatest concern to inform the sorrowing friends that his efforts are utterly unavailing, that the poor tormented soul is not a step nearer deliverance. Worked up by this time to considerable anxiety and distress, they then offer something more, and the priest resumes his prayers. But in a little while he stops again, declaring that the sum of money is yet too small. The offer is increased, and again the incantations proceed. Very likely the priest makes another and another pause before the spirit is declared free, each time dragging more and more out of the unfortunate relatives, who frequently become so excited that they tear the rings from their fingers and the bangles from their arms and give them to their greedy priests. When a large sum of money has thus been extorted from a family, the priests generally allow them to rest for a little while, but when they think the embarrassment has been got over, they are pretty certain to discover another who is crying to his relatives for relief."

"That is just the way the Roman Catholic priests go on with their people, isn't it, mother?" said Mabel. "They get a lot of money out of them by promising to say masses for the dead, don't they? But I did not know any but the Romanists believed in purgatory. I thought that was quite a popish idea, not a heathen one."

"It is curious how many points of resemblance

there are between Romanism and Buddhism," said Mrs. Foster. " The Romanists themselves have been puzzled by it, and one of their early Chinese missionaries declared that Buddhism must have been the rival system and master-plot of Satan to hinder the progress of the Christian faith. The principal Buddhist goddess is represented with a child in her arms, and is called the Queen of Heaven. Then the Buddhists, too, have monasteries and convents, their priests are not allowed to marry, and they have shaven crowns, they place candles on their altars, they use incense and rosaries, they tinkle bells and intone their prayers. One would have imagined that the Romanists would not have found it difficult to make converts among a people whose worship so much resembles their own, but though they have been working in China on and off for about 600 years, they seem to have made very few genuine *converts*. It is true that the Chinese Roman Catholics number somewhere about 800,000, but almost the whole of this number have been brought up from infancy in the Roman Catholic religion, and cannot be spoken of as converts from heathenism at all. The Roman Catholic missionaries have devoted themselves very much to the rescue of the poor little babies whom the Chinese throw out to die. These unfortunate little creatures are placed in homes and brought up by nuns, and of course their religion is as much one of education as that of the Buddhists around them."

"Do people ever go and see the Buddhist monasteries?" inquired one of the children. "Will the monks let people in?"

"Oh yes," replied Mrs. Foster, "they do not seem to mind inspection at all, but to be quite willing to show all there is to be seen. One of the most celebrated monasteries is at a place called Honam, an island in the Canton river. It occupies several acres of ground, and about 200 years ago was richly endowed by a Tartar prince. It is capable of maintaining 300 priests, but there are seldom as many as that living there. The temple—or rather temples, for there seem to be a great many—occupy the centre, and on either side are buildings containing the cells of the monks, the kitchens and dining-rooms. In one of these kitchens there is an enormous boiler, in which the priests, during times of scarcity, cook dinners for the poor, composed, I suppose, of vegetables, for they think it wrong to eat meat. Probably their belief in the transmigration of souls is the cause of this, but, whatever it may be, the strict Buddhists scrupulously avoid taking animal life. Of course it must be rather uncomfortable to eat meat when you never can feel sure that the butcher has not dislodged the soul of some dear relation in providing you with your dinner. The priests of Honam seem to take pigs under their particular protection, maintaining twelve of the most enormous creatures you can imagine, in the greatest possible comfort and plenty. These pigs are considered sacred, and when one dies another is immediately found to take its place. Every honour is paid to them, as a kind of reparation for the ills which their brethren suffer at the hands of men; and some of them live to a good old age—fifty, sixty, or even seventy years. These beasts and their beautifully clean styes are quite one of the sights of the place. Another thing which the monks show is the burial place. In the centre of this is a mausoleum, in which are preserved the ashes of those priests whose bodies are burnt. Some apparently prefer burial to cremation, and their graves are placed round this stone sepulchre."

"What sort of men are the priests?" said Frank Mason. "Are they learned sort of fellows?"

"No," replied Mrs. Foster, "generally they are a very low set, many of them outlaws and bandits, and very few of them at all educated. All the learned men, as I told you before, are Confucianists, and therefore of course will have nothing to do with Buddha. According to tradition, it was extremely difficult to get any priests at all when Buddhism was first introduced into the country. Many submitted to capital punishment rather than become priests to an idol, and at last the Emperor, in despair, offered a pardon to any felons who would undertake the service. Of course men flocked in then, and their low origin is said to have been the cause of the tonsure being assumed. Their heads were shorn in order to render them more easily recognized if they should make an attempt to escape."

"But what sort of places are the temples themselves?" inquired Tom. "You did not tell us that, mother."

"The central one is the principal, and in it there are three gigantic idols twelve feet in height and overlaid with gold. All the buildings are substantial and internally very splendid. There are immense numbers of idols, of different shapes and sizes, as well as a great many drums, lamps, and bells."

"Do the monks dress at all like the Roman Catholic ones?" asked one of the children.

"As to the cut of their garments, I cannot tell

you," replied Mrs. Foster; " I only know that they are made of grey cloth. The nuns, of whom there are altogether somewhere about 1,000, wear a long black robe, and have their heads completely shorn.

"But I think I have told you enough about Buddhism. I will tell you now about the Taouists. Lau-tzu, its founder, lived about the same time as Confucius, so that you see the sect is a very old one. Lau-tzu's god seems to have been Nature, but some centuries after his death Lau-tzu himself was turned into a god and worshipped under the name of a Shang-ti, two other gods being associated with him, and also called Shang-ti. By degrees the Taouist pantheon became very large. There are the star gods, the gods of heaven, earth, and water, the god and goddess of thunder, the god of war, and the god of wealth, and, I fancy, many others. But the god who seems to be thought most about by the people is one whom they call Yuh-hwang. Who or what he was I cannot tell you, but he seems most nearly to have usurped the place of the true God. In many respects Taouism, though an older religion than Buddhism, is now a mere copy of it. The priests are, on the whole, rather a better set of men than the Bonzes, and are not so much despised by the literary men. It is a very curious thing that many of the educated classes, who of course are all Confucianists by

THE GOD OF WATER.

profession, are practically Buddhists or Taouists. This, I think, shows how strong is the natural desire of every one to worship something. The Confucianist's own religion gives him very vague and indefinite ideas of

THE GOD OF THUNDER.

God, and discourages any near approach to Him; and, therefore, from the mere desire to satisfy the soul's yearning after God, he worships Buddha, although theoretically he abhors idolatry.

"Are the Chinese idols as hideous as those of India?" inquired Mabel.

"I scarcely know," answered Mrs. Foster, "but I should fancy not. The artistic skill of the Chinese is so much greater than that of the Hindoos that they are scarcely likely to worship such monsters of ugliness. Here is a picture of the thunder God, and from it you will see that, though terrific enough, there is nothing so utterly revolting as is often found in the Hindoo idols. The figure is emblematic, the wings representing swiftness, the chin terminating in an eagle's beak, and the eagle-like claws being intended to show the destructive nature of the storm. Sometimes this is even more forcibly expressed by animals lying dead beneath the god, and trees lying uprooted. But there is one Taouist god which I forgot to mention to you. This is an unpleasant kind of deity, that is supposed to live in people's kitchens, and to check the gossip of the women as they cook the people's dinners. This god is supposed to report on the conduct of the whole household at the close of each day.

"But, besides all the gods of which I have told, there are a number of others which can be classed neither as Buddhist nor Taouist. They are, as it were, native gods, and are treated with equal respect by both Buddhist and Taouist. Such is the earth-god, which is invoked whenever any new building is begun; the dragon-king, that is prayed to in the time of any flood or drought; the god who gives people children; the god who presides over small-pox; the god who watches over the illnesses of little children, and many others. In fact, every trade has its presiding deity."

"Do the Taouists have monasteries like the Buddhists?" said Grace; "and do they patronize pigs too."

"Not that I know of. The sacred pigs are an institution, I fancy, peculiar to the monastery at Honam. But the Taouists have monasteries, though the priests are not so numerous as those of Buddha. The principal mark by which they may be distinguished from the Bonzes is a peculiar tuft in which their hair is bound at the top of their heads."

"Are there Buddhists in any other part of the world besides China?" asked some one.

"Sad to say," replied Mrs. Foster, "it is a religion which reckons an enormous number of people in its ranks. It prevails in further India, Japan, Ceylon, Mongolia, Thibet, and the Corea. At one time, too, it was the religion of India, in which, as I said before, it had its rise. I think I have really told you quite enough about it, but one legend about its origin you will perhaps like to hear. It is a tradition of the Buddhists of Ceylon. They say that Brahma, having created the world, retired again into himself, and left his work to stand or fall as might be; Sceva, the destroyer, then took possession of it, and soon reduced it to a miserable condition. He trampled down man and beast, and ruined the fruits of the ground. Soon he would have utterly destroyed it, had not the gentle Vishnoo interfered, and, becoming incarnate, delivered it several times. But, in spite of Vishnoo's efforts, Sceva's armies still wasted and destroyed, until at last things were reduced to such a state that the air was so full of devils, there was not room to put a needle between them. Then Buddha, in compassion for the miseries of the human race, descended, and so far thinned the air of its horrible inhabitants that the sun was once more able to shine upon the world, and the fresh air to blow upon it."

"Are there any other religions in China besides those you have told us about?" said Tom.

"There are a good many Mahometans in some

districts, and round Ningpo there is a curious sect of people whose principal religious observance seems to consist in holding the breath as long as possible. They do it until the face becomes livid and the body stiff."

"Whatever good do they think it does?" exclaimed several of the children at once.

"They believe that while the breath is thus suspended, the spirit wanders about in the spirit-world in search of knowledge. Unfortunately, however, sometimes it wanders so far that it refuses to return."

"You mean the people die?" said Tom. "What idiots they must be! I cannot think how people can take such absurd notions into their heads, or how they can ever find people ridiculous enough to believe them, especially clever people like the Chinese."

"They seem absurd to us," replied Mrs. Foster, "because we have the Bible, and have been taught the truth about God and eternity from the time we could understand anything. But they only show how unable man is to find out God without a revelation, and the follies and absurdities of the religions that I have been telling you about ought to make us all very thankful that we were born English people, not Chinese, and ought to make us do all we can to send them the gospel."

CHAPTER III.

SOME CHINESE WONDERS.

A MONTH had passed away, and the bright busy little party had again gathered "to work for the niggers," as Tom always would express it, much to the indignation of his sisters.

"One would think you did not know that the negroes live in Africa, not in India," said Grace. "It is a great shame to talk as if little Mary Ray had thick lips, and woolly hair, and a horrid flat nose, instead of being the pretty child that she looks in her photograph."

Mary Ray was a little child in one of the mission schools in India whom the juvenile working party at The Bingle supported by the sale of their work. From time to time the lady who superintended the school sent the young workers accounts of their protégée, and, every now and then, she herself wrote them a short letter. One had arrived from her that very morning, and of course it had to be read, and handed round, and admired before the children were ready to listen to Mrs. Foster's talk about China.

"I tell you what, Mabel," said Tom, after every letter and word had been well examined and criticized, "if such a lot of us fellows take to making things, you will have to tip Mary Ray overboard, and take up a boy instead. It is a shame that we should be working for a girl."

"Oh, oh, Tom," said his mother, "what a shockingly unchivalrous speech! I am really quite ashamed. You ought to think yourself very much honoured by being allowed to do anything for a young lady; but if you are too small to appreciate the honour, you had better take up a boy in *addition*, not *instead* of little Mary Ray. I have no doubt it would be very easy to hear of one. Perhaps Mary Ray has a brother, or we might find a little Chinese who would be very glad to be taken into a nice school."

"That would be best, I think," said Tom; "because then there would be something different in the letters about them. If the Chinese have competitive examinations, I suppose they like their children to be taught, and have schools of their own, haven't they?"

"Yes, learning is held in high honour, and there are

schools for boys, though the poor girls are not thought worth the trouble of teaching."

"What a shame!" exclaimed Grace; "but what are boys' schools like?"

"Well, they are rather more fit for parrots than children, I fancy. The children learn long lessons by heart, but are not taught to think much about what they learn. They repeat their lessons standing with their backs to their masters, which we should think extremely rude. But I suppose they don't consider it so, for Chinese children are taught to treat their elders with great respect, and would not be allowed to do anything rude while in school. Schoolmasters are treated with special honour."

"Perhaps the Chinese children are very fond of peeping at the book if they stand with their faces towards it," suggested one of the children, "and that is the reason that they are made to stand the other way."

"I believe it is so," replied Mrs. Foster. "I should have thought it would have done just as well to have made the child stand a good way off, but perhaps Chinese books can be read at a long distance. It is a very funny language, you know, and a very difficult one to learn. It is what is called a pictorial language. That is to say, instead of having letters to spell the words, there is a picture or figure for each word. There is therefore no alphabet. Each word has to be learnt separately. These figures, too, are not simple things like our letters, which may be easily distinguished one from another, but are most complicated, composed, some of them, of fifteen or twenty strokes and dots, and yet at the same time many of them in general appearance so much alike that it is difficult to distinguish them. I am sure some of you little girls who find it so hard to know the German capitals apart, would soon be in despair if you were set to learn Chinese. Think what it would be to have to learn 5,000 or 6,000 German G's and S's! and yet that is the number of characters that it is necessary to know in order to be able to read the Bible fluently."

"What a fearful business!" exclaimed Tom; "I can't think how any one ever learns to read. I should have thought it was a simple impossibility. Why don't they give up such a bungling sort of way of doing things, and have an alphabet like other nations?"

"I really cannot tell you," replied Mrs. Foster. "But this pictorial language has one advantage which an alphabetical language would not possess. It is understood all over the Chinese empire. There are 200 spoken dialects, many of them as distinct from one another as Dutch from German, or German from English, so that in travelling from one part of the country to another, a Chinese may not in the least understand what the people say around him. Yet, if he knows how to read and write well he will always be able to make himself understood by other educated Chinese."

"That must be very convenient, certainly," said Mabel. "I suppose, in fact, written Chinese is a kind of thing that would do for any language, and could be read in English, or French, or German, just as well as in Chinese, if only English or French or Germans chose to take the trouble to learn it?"

"Yes," said Mrs. Foster, "I do not see why it should not. It might be employed as a kind of universal means of making one's self understood just in the same way as we employ the numerals. But the labour of learning it is so great that it would never be worth while. One missionary, who has lived in China for a good many years, speaks of it requiring two lifetimes to master it thoroughly."

"I cannot think how any one ever makes up his mind to be a missionary in China," said Mabel.

"What a business it must have been to translate the Bible! It has been done, hasn't it?"

"Yes; I saw a copy of it—or rather a part of it—at a missionary meeting not long ago. It seems to be a very bulky affair, so I suppose the language will not allow of very small print. It must, as you say, Mabel, have been a tremendous labour, but once done, you see, it does for the whole of China, and for Japan, too."

"Are the languages which the people speak very difficult?" inquired Frank Mason.

"Yes, extremely difficult," said Mrs. Foster; "so difficult that few missionaries ever master more than one dialect. The pronunciation is a serious difficulty, many of the sounds being utterly unknown to Europeans. But the tones are, I suppose, the greatest difficulty of all. In some dialects there are four tones, each of which is subdivided, and the meaning of the words depend upon the right use of these tones. The difference is often so extremely minute, that without an exceedingly good ear it is impossible to master them thoroughly. Some of the very best missionaries never have been able to accomplish it. And yet most ludicrous mistakes of course arise from the use of wrong tones. When the baptismal service was being translated, the missionary who did it was very much surprised to find that in every place where he thought he had said 'water,' the Chinese to whom he had been dictating had written 'book.' The mistake arose from the missionary saying the word with a wrong tone.

"In fact, there is scarcely any resemblance between Chinese and any other language in the world; and another very strange thing is the way in which the language remains the same. The Chinese of the present day speak almost exactly the same language as their ancestors did in Abraham's time. Of course, some new words have been introduced, but the old ones have remained unchanged; and though the country has been conquered two or three times, we find no trace of the conquest in the language."

"Did not the Tartars conquer the country?" asked one of the boys. "We had something about it, I know, in a geography lesson not long ago. Let me see. The Great Wall was built in order to keep them out, wasn't it, but they got over it and conquered it? Won't you tell us about the Great Wall, Mrs. Foster? It is tremendously big, isn't it, and very old?"

"Yes," replied Mrs. Foster, "it is, I suppose, one of the greatest wonders in the world. How or when it was built it is impossible to determine, but apparently

D

it is pretty certain that it was completed 2,000 years ago. It is about 1,500 miles long, and extends over the most diversified country; now down in valleys, and now over mountain-tops. One of the ridges over which it extends is more than 5,000 feet high, and how the materials of which it was formed were brought to the spot is as great a mystery as the construction of the pyramids in Egypt. For you must not think of it as a mere wall. It is a regular fortification, with towers or bastions every hundred yards; and it is all so massive and well-built that though some of the outworks have fallen into decay the mass of the wall is still perfect. It is built of a blue kind of brick, and there are, in some places, remains of what appear to have been the brick-kilns in which the bricks were baked. Another very curious thing about this wall is, that in it there are marks which look, to those who understand such things, as if the Chinese made use of something very like field-pieces in the defence of their country. Of course, if these marks are what clever people think them to be, it is evident that the Chinese say no more than the truth when they claim to have discovered gunpowder long before it was thought of in Europe."

"Don't you think, mother," said Tom, "that it was rather a mad idea to imagine that a wall would keep people out if they felt disposed to come over it? The wall itself would surely never do it, it would want an immense number of soldiers to defend it."

"Well, I suppose it did," replied Mrs. Foster; "more than the Chinese could supply for the Manchoo Tartars came over at last. But it helped very materially in the defence of the country for 1,600 years. No wall, I suppose, ever will keep a superior enemy out of a country. It only delays the day of conquest."

"Is the Great Wall very broad and high?" asked Mabel.

"I suppose both height and breadth vary, but in some parts it is thirty feet high, and thirty feet broad, big enough, you see, to prove a serious obstacle in the way of an advancing army."

"I can't conceive how it was built," said Tom; "it seems to me as if people in old times were fond of doing things to puzzle those who live afterwards. Stonehenge is a perfect problem, isn't it? Nobody can imagine how such immense stones could ever have been got on to Salisbury Plain, and the idea of carrying the things for such a monstrous wall up 5,000 feet seems perfectly absurd. Yet there is the wall, and it couldn't have grown, so somebody must have done it. Then, too, what an enormous time, or else, what an enormous number of men, it must have taken to build a wall of such an immense length. How do you think it was done, mother?"

"I should think that, probably, the emperor made the work compulsory, that people had to work at it, whether they liked it or not; in fact, that he levied workmen much in the same way as Solomon did for the building of the temple, or, perhaps, he may have employed some large slave population on the work, just as Pharaoh employed the children of Israel in the building of his treasure-cities."

"But the Great Wall, you must remember, is only one of the wonders of China. The great canal is almost equally wonderful. It is of immense length— nearly 700 miles long, in fact is the longest canal ever constructed. It is deep and wide enough to admit large vessels, and is of great service as a line of communication, for it connects the two rivers, the Yiang-tze-kiang and the Yellow River. It is very useful, too, in draining swampy districts. I met with rather an interesting description of it the other day in an old account of an embassy which was sent from England towards the end of the last century. I will try and tell you all that I think will interest you. Canals in England, you know, are generally made as straight as

A SLUICE ON THE GRAND CANAL.

possible, narrow, and pretty much the same width all the way. But the Grand Canal of China is winding in its course, and very irregular in point of width, sometimes being quite wide. It is so constructed, too, as to have a current, and altogether is, I should fancy, much more like a river than any European canal. It has no locks, but the flow of water is regulated by flood-gates of the very simplest construction. Piers of stone project from either bank of the canal, leaving just room enough between them to admit the passage of a vessel, and into grooves cut in these piers a few planks are let down. You can imagine that such flood-gates as these do not cost much to keep in repair, but it requires some skill to direct the vessels through them without accident. For this purpose an immense oar is made to project from the bow, and one of the crew conducts her with the greatest nicety. Men, too, are stationed on each pier with things made of skin stuffed with hair, which they let down between the vessel and the stone.

"The flood-gates are not opened whenever any vessel wants to go through, but only at stated hours, and each vessel has to pay a toll.

"The highest part of the canal is at the spot where the river Luen falls into it. This is the largest river by which the canal is fed, and it falls into it with a rapid stream in a line which is almost perpendicular to the course of the canal. In order, no doubt, to prevent it washing away the opposite bank, and to make it take the course of the canal, a strong bulwark of stone has been built, and as the waters of the river strike this bulwark, they divide, and part of them follow the northern course of the canal, and part the southern.

"The embassy, as they went along this canal, were a source of great interest to the people living near its shores. Whenever they were near a town, crowds of people collected to gaze at them, and on one occasion they were the innocent cause of an accident. They were passing down a part of the canal on which a number of barges were drawn up at the sides, and in their eagerness to gaze at the white foreigners, the people crowded on to these. The projecting stern of one of them gave way under its weight, and a good many people fell into the water. The author of the account forgets to tell us whether any of them were drowned, though he says there was a great deal of shrieking and struggling; and apparently the cause of his forgetfulness was his astonishment at the coolness with which the spectators took the danger of their fellow-countrymen. It did not seem in the least to disturb them, or to distract their attention from the

ECONOMY OF TIME AND LABOUR.

passing spectacle, and though one boat did row out to the rescue, the man in it was much more eager to secure a hat which was floating away, than to save its unfortunate owner."

"Are the Chinese cruel then?" asked one of the little girls.

"I fear we must at any rate give them the character of being very selfish and unfeeling. The children, as I told you before, are trained to treat their parents with the greatest respect and reverence—in fact almost to worship them, both living and dead, but I am afraid the Chinaman cares little about any but his relations.

"However, there is another thing that I must tell you about this voyage of the embassy. On their passage down the canal, they passed the place where the fishing birds of China are bred, and on a large lake near by saw a number of birds engaged in their work. These birds are a kind of cormorant, a brown bird with a white throat, a rounded tail, blue eyes, and yellow bill. They are set to fish from a small boat or raft, and of these boats or rafts there were hundreds on the lake. On each boat there were eight or ten birds, and it was amusing to see them at a signal from their owner all plunge into the water. Sometimes they returned with an enormous fish, and they were so well trained that it was quite unnecessary to take any measures to prevent their swallowing any part of their prey. They were always quite content with the morsels which their masters gave them. I cannot say whether

this is always the case. They may have been particularly good birds, for I am sure that in some accounts of these funny fishermen I have seen it stated that a ring is usually placed around their throats in order to render it impossible for them to eat what they catch."

"But I do not see why that should be necessary,"

said Mabel? "Dogs can be trained not to touch the game which they assist in killing, and I suppose hawks used to be taught to bring down other birds without eating them. Why should it not be the same with the fishing cormorant? But the Chinese have some other funny way of fishing, haven't they? Some contrivance with a board, I think it is."

"I know what you mean," replied Mrs. Foster. "A board painted white is fixed to the side of a boat, the edge inclining towards the water. On moonlight nights the boat is so placed that the moon shines on this painted board, and the rays of light striking on its whitened surface make it look as if it were moving water. The fishes are deceived and jump upon it. The boatman then immediately raises the board with a string and turns the fish into the boat."

"Are not the Chinese very fond of fishing," said Frank? "It seems to me that if you hear or read about China there is sure to be something about the different ways in which the people catch fish."

"Quite true," replied Mrs. Foster. "The reason is just this: the population of China is very great, and its animal resources very small, so that fish is a very important article of food. The common people among the Chinese scarcely ever taste meat such as we eat, beef or mutton, unless it is the flesh of animals that have died of some disease or accident. But though they can understand there being some reason for not eating meat at all, and the strict Buddhists do abstain from animal food, they cannot see any reason why you should prefer one animal to another. They make no distinction whatever between clean and unclean meat, and would just as soon eat dog or donkey, as beef or mutton. In fact the poor feed upon the most filthy things, and seldom enjoy anything so good as bow-wow. Earth-worms, rats, mice, the heads and feet of fowl, and sea reptiles of all kinds, are greedily devoured by them. Frogs of course they eat, but we must not exclaim at that when such a refined people as the French keep them in countenance. Such is the food of the poor, but I do not know that the dainties of the rich would be much more to our taste. One of the things most highly esteemed are the bird's nests, which are imported from some of the East India Islands. They are the nests of a kind of swallow, and are made into soup which tastes rather like a sickly kind of vermicelli. Sharks' fins are another great delicacy, and fetch a high price when properly prepared. The *bêche de la mer*, too, a horrible looking sea-slug, is a great favourite with the gourmands of China.

The Marquis de Beauvoir, a French nobleman who travelled in China a few years ago, gives a most amusing account of a dinner of which he partook while in the country. I will tell you what were some of the dishes. There were sharks' fins with a kind of glue sauce, hashed dog with lotus sauce, birds'-nest soup, sinews of whale with sugar sauce, dried fish and rat croquettes, sharks'-fat soup, stewed starfish, and fresh-water tadpoles. He tells the friend to whom he sends the description, that with a large quantity of gelatine, some giblets of fowls, and the sweepings of a druggist's shop, he thinks he could produce something which would give a very good idea of a Chinese dinner."

"Is not the wine which the Chinese drink very funny stuff too," said Tom. "I remember hearing Captain Cooper say so when he came back from China."

"The Marquis de Beauvoir seems to have thought it much upon a par with the eatables. He says there were two wines at his dinner, one a pink wine, which tasted like medicine, and another very sickening one, made from rice. But I suppose in the matter of these wines, as of everything else, tastes differ, for in another book of travels I find this rice wine described as not at all unpleasant. It is drunk warm from small cups.

The Chinese have a funny custom when they drink any one's health. They bow to one another as we do, but hold the cup in both hands as they drink, and then each turns the inside of it towards his friend, in order that he may see that the contents have been fairly drunk. It is considered most uncourteous to leave any at the bottom.

"No doubt you all know that the Chinese use chopsticks at their meals, instead of knives and forks. But very likely you do not know what chopsticks are like. They are just two pieces of wood or ivory, about the thickness of a goose-quill, and nine or ten inches long. I expect we should find them very troublesome things to eat with, but there is nothing like habit, and the Chinese probably find them just as convenient as our more elaborate implements. For rice,—and you know they consume great quantities of that,—they hold the basin containing it quite close to the chin with one hand, and with the chopsticks, which they hold in the other, shovel the grains into the mouth. I should think it cannot be a very elegant operation, but I suppose they see nothing ugly in it. For fish, meat, and vegetables, they use the chopstick like a pair of tongs, and most dexterously manage to get the food into their mouths."

"Don't you think they must be very difficult things to learn to use," said one of the girls. "I pity the poor children. A knife and fork are always hard enough for little things to manage, or even a spoon. They generally mess their faces terribly, and I can't think how they get anything to eat at all when they have to use chopsticks. But won't you tell us something about the women and girls now, Mrs. Foster? I want very much to know what they are like, and how they spend their time."

"I think I must not begin to talk about them to-day," Mrs. Foster replied. "For it is time that we put the work away. But I will tell you all I know next time."

CHAPTER IV.

GIRLS AND WOMEN.

MRS. FOSTER did not forget her promise. When the work was all arranged at the next meeting, when everybody knew exactly what to do, when the boys had their glue-pot, their cardboard, and their colours, and the girls their needles, scissors, and pins, Mrs. Foster began :—

"The first thing I have to tell you about the Chinese girls is a very sad thing, and it is this, that a great many of them are killed when they are tiny babies."

"But, mamma," said Mabel, "did not Captain Cooper say the other day that the infanticide in China is very much exaggerated?"

"He did say so," replied Mrs. Foster; "and I find that some books about China confirm his statement, so that I hope he is not altogether mistaken. Still, though it may not be a crime so generally practised as has sometimes been supposed, it is, I fear, fearfully common. As far as I can gather, it is more generally practised in the country villages than in the large towns; and this may account for the difference of opinion on the matter which we find to exist in the books of those who have written about it. Yet even in the large towns, it may chance at once to come before even the passing stranger. The Marquis de Beauvoir, in just taking a walk outside the city of Canton, stumbled upon no less than seven dead or dying babies. One had been stabbed with a knife; another had, apparently, been thrown over the wall, for some of its bones were broken; some were completely frozen; and all were too far gone to leave any chance of their lives being saved. The sight was most heart-rending, and the Marquis says that it was a long time before he could get the thought of those miserable babies out of his mind, or their wailing cry out of his ears. But probably these infants had—some of them, at any rate—been left in the hope that some charitable person might pick them up and adopt them; for this is not the common method of committing the horrid crime. It is generally the poor who destroy their little girls; and the difficulty of providing food for a large family is, probably, the reason. A missionary, who some years ago took great trouble to find out all he could about the matter, was told in one village that the poor there generally put to death two out of every four daughters. In the next village they said the same, only adding that sometimes the proportion of those murdered was even greater, occasionally only one daughter out of six being allowed to live. But the people said it altogether depended on the poverty of the parents. They described the way in which the poor little things were usually murdered, and said that it was done either by drowning, pinching the throat, suffocating by putting a wet cloth over the mouth, or by choking with a few grains of rice. This missionary met with one man who said he had had eight children, but they were all girls, and he had murdered five. He had a little baby girl in his arms at the time, of which he seemed very fond, and there seemed no want of parental affection about him. He pitied himself a great deal, and bemoaned his hard fate in having had so many daughters and no son, and said that both he and his wife wept a great deal when they killed a child, and were very miserable for ten days. But it never seemed to occur to him that there was anything wrong in the act. In Canton there is a large Foundling Hospital, supported by voluntary contributions, intended for the female children of those who are too poor to maintain their families, and probably this is the reason why infanticide is not so common there as in other parts of the country."

"It is the missionaries who have set up this Foundling Hospital, I suppose," said Grace.

"Not the one I am referring to now," replied Mrs. Foster. "It is maintained by the pagan natives, and is particularly worth noticing on that account. Two hundred babies are said to be annually received into it. At the entrance there is a little box, in which the baby is placed, and then a bell is rung to let the people inside know of its arrival. A great many of the babies are put out to nurse, the institution paying the women who take care of them; and each of these children has a wooden tally, with its own name and that of the institution upon it, which is kept by the nurse. It has often been said that no heathen religion has ever supplied a motive strong enough to produce works of benevolence, and I suppose China is the only country where this is not strictly true. It can boast of this hospital, and also of another institution, called 'The Hall of United Benevolence,' which supplies coffins and the expenses of burial for the unclaimed dead, and also furnishes relief to some old and infirm persons."

"But do not the missionaries try to save the little babies, too?" asked one of the children.

"Yes," replied Mrs. Foster. "I will tell you, by-and-by, about one missionary lady who has saved a great many poor little things, who would otherwise have perished; but now I want to tell you a little about the condition of the Chinese girls whose parents are well off, and who are therefore allowed to live. Occasionally a rich Chinese will teach a favourite daughter; but it is not by any means considered a matter of necessity for girls to be taught anything beyond the art of cooking, making shoes, and doing plain needlework and embroidery. Of course, even this small amount of teaching is more than falls to the lot of the young ladies of India, and gives them the power of occupying their time; yet it is melancholy to think of their minds being left wholly uncultivated. Perhaps some of you little girls think it must be rather nice to have no troublesome French exercises or verbs to learn; but I think none of you would like not to be able to read. Yet few Chinese girls have the opportunity of learning, for there are no girls' schools in any part of the Empire. But though the Chinese girl's mind is not considered worth cultivating, some pains are bestowed upon her body. As soon as she is five years old it is considered quite time to prevent her feet growing any more; for little feet are considered a great beauty."

"And don't you think they are pretty?" exclaimed a little girl, her eyes very wide open with amazement at the thought that any one could doubt such a generally received opinion. The truth was, that this little girl was rather vain of her own pretty little feet, and, as her young companions were quite aware of her weakness, they could not forbear smiling at her almost involuntary exclamation. Poor Lucy saw the smile, and bent low over her work to hide the blush which suffused her face.

"Very pretty indeed, I think they are, Lucy," said Mrs. Foster, "when they are not so small as to be out of proportion to the rest of the figure. But I have seen people, even in England, whose feet were too small to be pretty; and I always think it not only silly, but wrong, to wear shoes that are too small, with the idea of improving one's appearance. Few things are more miserable than tight shoes; and yet the suffering caused by them must be a mere trifle compared to what the Chinese girls have to endure. The great toe is allowed to keep its natural position, but the others are made to turn under, and are tightly bandaged. At the early age of five the poor little things can see no reason for submitting to such very painful treatment, if they can possibly avoid it, and it requires the utmost vigilance of their mothers to make them keep the bandages on. Of course their feet are of very little use to them, and at the beginning of the process they cannot walk at all without being supported. They always walk in an uncertain and tottering manner. The torture, too, of such treatment must necessarily injure the constitution; and yet all, except the very poor, submit more or less to this monstrous custom."

"But whatever can be the reason that such a custom ever arose?" inquired Grace.

"It is difficult to say," replied Mrs. Foster. "Some have imagined that it was forced upon them by their husbands and fathers, in order to prevent their going out of doors. But it seems scarcely likely that this can have been the case, for the women of China are allowed much more liberty than those of India or Turkey, and yet no such barbarous custom is known in either of those countries. One story is, that the daughter of an emperor was once born with dwarfed feet, and that the ladies of the court took to limping and compressing their feet in imitation. The fashion spread from the court to the towns, and from the towns to the country, until what was only a fashion became an established custom. But, whatever may have been its origin, certain it is that it is so completely considered a mark of degradation to have feet of a reasonable size that, if one of two sisters, perfectly alike in every other respect, were to have her feet neglected, she would be considered unfit for the other to associate with, and would be treated like a servant."

"But what does the foot look like, mamma, when it is stunted in this way? Is it the natural shape, only smaller?"

"No," said Mrs. Foster; "all the beauty of the form is lost, and it becomes a mere shapeless stump. And yet, so beautiful does it appear to the Chinese, that they think the shoes which cover it cannot be too elaborate; and they very often heighten the appearance of deformity by making the heel project two inches backwards beyond the foot. Another of the doubtful beauties of a Chinese lady is her long nails. Those on her left hand she allows to grow until they are like bird's claws, as a mark that she is a lady, and not obliged to do anything. The right hand nails she is forced to keep rather shorter, in order that she may be able to embroider. The long nails, though, are not peculiar to ladies. A missionary tells of having seen a schoolmaster who could boast of one six inches long."

"How disgusting!" exclaimed Mabel. "But I cannot imagine how any one could keep such a thing. I should have thought it would be sure to break. I should think a man with such a nail as that certainly could not do much. The care needed by such a treasure must occupy all his time and attention. But tell us something now, mamma, about the weddings of the Chinese. As the women are allowed to go about more than in India, I suppose the people do not have to marry husbands and wives whom they have not seen."

"Probably not; but there is often no intercourse before the wedding, I fancy. I met with a very amusing story the other day of a mistake in the matter of a wedding, which could not possibly have arisen in any country where marriages are arranged as we arrange them in England. A certain gentleman named Sing, finding himself in a position to support a wife, set to work to look about for one. A very beautiful young lady, who took part in a procession to some idol temple, caught his eye, and he made up his mind to try and win her. He knew that she was the daughter of a neighbouring gentleman, and thought he had ascertained that she was the fifth. A ching-jin, or go-between, was employed, and the match was arranged."

"What sort of person is that?" said Tom.

"Generally an elderly lady," replied his mother, and her business is to manage the exchange of presents and settle the terms of the engagement. In this case everything went smoothly, and the marriage-day arrived. The bride was carried, with all the usual pomp, in a gaily decorated sedan chair, and accompanied by a band of musicians, to the house of the bridegroom. When she reached it she was, according to the Chinese fashion, lifted over the threshold by two matrons, and presented to her future husband. The marriage knot was just about to be tied by the solemn drinking of what is called "the cup of alliance," when poor Sing to his horror discovered that his would-be bride was not the beautiful girl whom he had fallen in love with, but a very plain creature deeply scarred with the small-pox. The fact was he had made a mistake. The daughter whom he had wished for was not the fifth, but the fourth. You can imagine the perplexity and mortification of his position. At first he wanted the young lady to go home again, but she seemed so distressed at the proposal that he at length good-naturedly made up his mind to make the best of his disappointment, and to put up with a plain bride instead of a pretty one. We must hope that he was rewarded by finding that if she was not handsome she was good."

"Do the Chinese dress very beautifully?" inquired one of the little girls; "and do the fashions keep altering there as they do in England?"

"No, not nearly as much. In fact, the dress of the ladies varies very little. Instead of under-linen, they wear a netting of silk, and over this a waistcoat and trousers of silk. When the weather is very cold these are generally lined with fur. Above these there is a long satin robe, gracefully fastened in at the waist with a sash. Of course, the dress varies in richness and beauty according to the means and circumstances of the wearer. Here is the attire of a bride, whom some missionaries were honoured with the sight of, a few days after her wedding. She wore a scarlet robe, superbly trimmed with gold, and this completely covered her from the shoulders to the ground. The sleeves of the robe were very full, and had a fringe of small bells. Her head-dress sparkled with jewels. She wore a kind of coronet of pearls, from the front of which hung over her forehead a brilliant angular ornament. For a Chinese, she was a nice-looking girl, and bore the ordeal of being looked at by strangers with composure and modesty. The missionaries were not introduced into her apartments, but she was directed to stand at the door, that they might get a view of her as they went by. She was surrounded by a number of old women, and one of these, determined that the English strangers should quite understand all the charms of a Chinese bride, raised the hem of the robe for a moment, that they might have a view of the perfection of her beauty, namely, her exceedingly small foot. It was reduced to a mere point at the toe, and her shoes, like the rest of her attire, were richly embroidered with gold."

"But I suppose the poor women cannot afford the luxury of small feet," said Grace. "Tell us something about them now, mamma."

"Of course it is only the rich who have the exceedingly small feet," said Mrs. Foster. "A tiny foot is considered a mark of gentility; but just as poor people in England ape the fashions of those who are better off, so the poor women of China do all they can to make their feet like those of their richer sisters. They cannot keep them so systematically bandaged as those who are not obliged to work, but they do all they can to stop their growth. There is, indeed, one province in the south where the custom does not prevail, and the women of that province are so robust and healthy that peasants come from other provinces to buy, as they say, a working wife. These women are certainly *working women*, and are sometimes employed by their husbands to do work which we only think fit for horses or oxen. A farmer has even been seen to drive his wife, yoked to the plough."

"What a brute!" exclaimed all the boys in a breath.

"Could not he be punished, mamma?" added Tom. "Surely such a thing no government would tolerate."

"A good many heathen governments would, I am afraid," said Mrs. Foster. "Nothing but the Bible ever teaches men to treat women properly; and certainly in China they are looked upon not only as the *weaker*, but as the *inferior* sex. While they are young the father, and when they are married the husband, can do pretty much what they like with them. Poor things! they are almost always despised, and as no pains are ever taken to draw out their powers and cultivate their minds, one cannot wonder at it. A highly educated man cannot, of course, long find much pleasure in the society of a woman who cannot read. As I told you just now, a Chinese considers it a heavy trial to have many daughters, and looks upon them as almost useless creatures. They cannot carry on his family name, or help to support him in his old age, and they cannot perform his funeral rites. At the age of sixteen they marry, and pass into another family, being, to all intents and purposes, bought from their parents, who henceforth frequently omit their names when enumerating the number of their children. And yet these poor despised women are of the greatest use. Beside rearing children and looking after the domestic affairs, they cultivate silk-worms, and are almost the sole weavers in the country.

"But now I think I must tell you a little about what has been done by Miss Aldersey for some of the poor Chinese girls. She was one of the very first people who engaged in missionary work in China. I dare say you may have heard that for a very long time it was almost impossible to carry the Gospel thither, for the Chinese would not have foreigners in the country. Indeed, it was not until 1858 that the country was thoroughly open, though in 1843 leave was granted to foreigners to enter the five ports of Canton, Amoy, Foo-chow, Ningpo, and Shanghae, and to go thirty miles inland from either of these places."

"Were there no missionaries at all in the country then?" inquired Mabel. "I thought I had heard something about a Dr. Morrison, who went there a long time ago."

"You are quite right. He did. He landed in Canton somewhere about 1807; but he did it at a risk, knowing that he might be sent away at any time. However, I do not want to tell you about him just now. Perhaps I may do that another time. As we have been talking so much about the women to-day, I want to tell you about Miss Aldersey and her girls.

"Miss Aldersey had a great desire to go to China when she was quite young. Indeed, she began to learn Chinese when she was only nineteen, and to prepare herself in every way that she could think of for the hardships which she knew that she would have to endure in the life which she hoped soon to enter upon. But just as she was preparing to start, a sad event made it most plainly her duty to give up the project for a time. A sister died quite suddenly, leaving six little children to be taken care of. No doubt it was a bitter disappointment to let her missionary friends sail without her; but she knew she could only expect a blessing when walking in the path of duty, and that that path lay now in England. So for six years she took care of her little nephews and nieces, doing her best to be like their own mother to them. At the end of that time they no longer needed her, and her thoughts and desires again turned to the Chinese children. No obstacle seemed now to stand in her way, and in 1837 she accompanied a missionary and his wife to the island of Java, where, you know, there are a great many Chinese. For five years she taught a school there, and then, accompanied by a young English girl, and followed by two of her Chinese scholars, she went to Singapore, and from thence, in 1843, proceeded to Ningpo, landing on the very day on which the treaty was signed which opened the five ports. She at once opened a boarding-school, and children rapidly flocked in, though, of course, she had many difficulties to contend with. The parents often looked upon her with suspicion, and were half afraid to let her have their girls. Once the rumour got abroad that she had murdered all her scholars, and one of the mothers came, in great alarm, and demanded to see her child. Of course she was at once produced, and when the woman saw that she was alive and well, she gravely asked her whether she had not been killed and brought to life again. But in spite of all troubles and vexations, a great blessing rested on Miss Aldersey's work, and the accounts which she has given of some of the girls is most interesting. I will tell you a little about one called San Avong. She was the eldest of four sisters, who were some of the earliest of Miss Aldersey's pupils, and was nine years old when she entered the school. The mother hesitated for some time before she could resolve to let Miss Aldersey have the charge of her daughters; for having once been present while a Bible lesson was being given, and having seen the quiet and order which prevailed among the children, she made up her mind that they were afraid of Miss Aldersey. At length, however, her fears, I suppose, having been dispelled in some way, she entered into a regular engagement to leave the children with Miss Aldersey for two, four, six, and eight years, according to their respective ages. San Avong, as I said, was the eldest, and therefore had only two years of regular teaching; but those two years were long enough for her to learn the folly of idolatry and the love of the Saviour. From the very first she was a child of great promise, and very soon it was evident her heart was given to the Lord Jesus. At the end of the two years she was taken from her studies, and married to a heathen. This was, of course, a bitter trial; but there was no help for it, and the poor child had to submit. However, Miss Aldersey did succeed in getting the idolatrous rites omitted which usually accompany a marriage, and also succeeded in extracting a promise from the relatives that San Avong should be allowed to spend the Sundays with her. This was a great comfort to poor San Avong; but on the very first Sunday after the marriage she was forcibly made to bow down before her husband's ancestral tablets. This caused her the greatest distress, and she would not be comforted until convinced that what she had done against her will could be no sin. After this, she had to endure a great deal of persecution, until Miss Aldersey hit upon a plan for her relief. She engaged the husband, Si Yang, as cook, and he allowed San Avong to return to the school, only stipulating that she should not learn English. Four years passed quietly away, and then Si Yang died. His friends and relatives declared that his death was owing to San Avong's conduct at the marriage; and out of revenge, I suppose, protested that she must be sold to pay his debts. Whether he really left any or not, I cannot tell; but, at any rate, Miss Aldersey produced the fifty dollars required, and San Avong was left in peace. She now devoted herself, with more energy and zeal than ever, to the work of the school, and soon became a most valuable teacher. She did what she could, too, out of doors, taking every opportunity that offered of talking to her countrywomen about the Saviour. At one time she held a weekly meeting in the town of Ningpo, and when Miss Aldersey paid visits to distant villages, San Avong went with her, and did what she could to help her in her work among the people. At last, Miss Aldersey, who was getting old, thought it better to turn her school over to the American missionaries. San Avong for a short time continued to teach in it; but soon rejoined her old friend, it being judged better that she should remain under her protection."

"What were they afraid would happen to her?" said Tom.

"That her friends might force her to marry a heathen. They, I suppose, had a good deal of respect for Miss Aldersey, and were less likely to make themselves disagreeable to San Avong while she was under her roof. So San Avong took charge of an infant school, and managed the little things so well that their mothers were quite astonished. After some years she did marry again; but this time it was of her own accord, and her husband was an excellent Christian man. He was a teacher, and used to go about the country preaching to the people. San Avong went with him, and did what she could; but on one of these tours she caught a severe cold, and her health gave way. Still, she worked to the very last, feeling, no doubt, that she could never do enough for her precious Saviour. Her heathen mother and sister gave her a good deal of trouble, telling her that her sickness was all owing to her new religion. But she was happy in all her sufferings, and strove to comfort her sorrowing friends. At length she gently passed away, and entered into that glorious rest prepared for the faithful soldiers of the cross."

CHAPTER V.

WRETCHEDNESS.

"I HAVE a question that I want to ask you about China, Mrs. Foster," said Frank Mason, when the busy workers were again assembled. "May I?"

"Certainly; and I will do my best to answer it, unless it should prove too difficult."

"I don't suppose it is difficult at all," said Frank. "It is just this. You said, you know, that there are such an immense number of people in China that really there is hardly enough for them all to eat; and that that is the reason why the people eat such filthy things, and why the poor people kill so many of their girls. Now, I want to know why the people stop in China. Why don't they emigrate, as so many people in England do? I suppose England would get too full if it was not for that."

"A proper kind of emigration would, doubtless, be a very good thing indeed for China; and I suppose now a great many Chinese do seek their fortunes in

other lands. But for a very long time anything of the kind was very much discouraged, and other nations were forbidden to traffic with the country, lest they should make the people discontented with their own land. There is now, however, a kind of emigration carried on, but it is of the most objectionable kind, and seems really almost to equal in its horrors the slave-trade itself. It is carried on principally by the Portuguese, and seems to me only a modified kind of slave-trade. The agents, by fair means or foul, persuade men to sell themselves for eight years, to work in the plantations of Cuba or the guano pits of Peru. Of course everything is painted to them in the most glowing colours, and the walls of the office in which contracts are made and signed are generally ornamented with pictures representing ship-loads of happy coolies on their way to what is described to them as a kind of Canaan. The Marquis de Beauvoir gives a long account of the matter, and he says the form of contract is just this:—
' I undertake to work twelve hours a day for eight years in the service of the holder of this contract, and to renounce all freedom during the time. My employer undertakes to feed me and to give me four piastres a month, to clothe me, and to set me free on the day of the expiration of the contract.' "

"I do not see that that is so very dreadful," said Tom. "It is only like engaging to work for one master for eight years; and that is what numbers of people do of their own free will."

"Yes, of their own free will; and that just makes all the difference. Many hired servants, as you say, stay more than eight years in one situation; but that is when their employers are kind and considerate. How would you like to have to work eight years for a cruel and tyrannical master? And yet that is what far too many of the poor coolies, as they are called, have to do. Of course, some may have the happy lot of being sold to kind people, and may, therefore, get through their time of servitude comfortably, and, when it is over, may work on their own account and make their fortunes; but those are the rare exceptions. As a rule, I fear they are a bad set of men who buy these poor fellows; and knowing they have them only for a short term of years, they get as much work as ever they can out of them, not scrupling to use any cruelty that will help them to attain their object. But there are many horrors through which the poor coolies have to pass before they arrive at their destination. Their passage across the ocean equals in its suffering that of the poor negroes. Indeed, so terrible is it, that not unfrequently they rise upon the crew and murder them; or, if the crew are strong enough to maintain the upper hand, they themselves are thrust down into the hold, and there suffocated."

"But I cannot think how they ever get fellows to go," said Tom, "if they treat them in that way."

"You may well wonder," replied Mrs. Foster; "but the fact is, that very few do go of their free will. They are, indeed, formally asked by the authorities whether any force has been put upon them; but the agents understand so thoroughly how to make a man's life a burden to him if he tells the truth and refuses to go, that, once in their clutches, very few Chinamen venture to do so."

"But how do they get into the agent's clutches in the first instance?" inquired Mabel.

"Well, the principal place where the trade is carried on is Macao, in the south. There have been of late years many internal wars in the southern provinces, and large numbers of the prisoners have been sold to the Portuguese traders. Then, too, Macao is a great place for gambling; and, as in all such places, there are many poor, wretched creatures who have ruined themselves and got deeply into debt. These are pressed hardly by their creditors, and they just sell themselves as the only means left to them of paying their debts."

"What a horrible sort of thing it seems altogether!" said Tom. "Has it been going on long?"

"Not very long, I believe; but certainly the whole thing is most iniquitous. The poor coolie generally sells himself for about £12; but when he arrives in Cuba his price has generally risen to about £70, and the difference between the £12 and the £70 is divided between the different persons concerned in the wretched trade. If the poor creatures are to sell themselves at all, they certainly ought to have the price they are worth."

"I wonder the English do not try to put a stop to the thing," said Frank, "as they do to the slave-trade."

"I should think it is probably a much more difficult matter to deal with, as there is an appearance of the men going by their own free will. But you will be glad to hear that it is entirely forbidden in the English colony of Hongkong. However, as I said before, a proper system of emigration would be the very best thing in the world for China; for the surplus population is so great, that the number of beggars is something frightful."

"Oh yes, I know," said Mabel. "I think I have

heard that before. Don't they often blind themselves, just to excite people's compassion?"

"Yes, I believe it is a very common plan, when they find they do not gain enough with sound eyes, to destroy them in the hopes of better success. A poor man once came to a medical missionary with eyes most frightfully inflamed, and the lids enormously swollen. He stated that he was a plasterer by trade, and that some lime had accidentally fallen into his eyes. However, on investigating the case, the missionary found that there was no accident in the matter, but that the man had intentionally put the lime into his eyes in order to produce blindness. He had perfectly succeeded, for the sight was completely destroyed. The pain had, however, been greater than he expected, and therefore he had come to the missionary for relief. It is, I believe, very common for parents, when they cannot quite make up their minds to part with their own sight, to put out the eyes of one or two of their children instead, either by inserting lime, as this man did, or by sticking a needle into them.

"But, after all, this is only one means among many others to which they resort for the purpose of exciting compassion. They maim themselves in all manner of ways. In the south part of the province of Shantung there are professional beggar-surgeons, who perform operations on their companions. Apparently, however, they are very bungling, and put their patients to the most unnecessary torture. Four men once presented themselves before some one, all having lost the lower part of their legs. The story they told was, that they had lost them in a fire; but it was rather a singular circumstance that the fire had burnt almost exactly the same piece off each leg. The truth, probably, was that they had been operated upon by one of these beggar-doctors. Their method of proceeding, apparently, is this: they tie a piece of string round the calf of the leg, drawing it tighter and tighter, until the lower part begins to mortify; then they saw through the bone, and fasten up the wound. What is the purpose of the preparatory torture of the string I am sure I do not know, or why they do not go boldly to work, and cut off the limb at once.

"There is, or was, one beggar who apparently was a notorious character; at least, I find him mentioned in different books. He used to sit in the tea-gardens of Shanghae, day after day, gazing at his own foot, which he kept, dried and withered, upon a stone before him. Whether it had been amputated in the way I have described, I cannot tell you. One author thinks it had, while another considers that it had dropped off from disease.

"But the Chinese do not always take the trouble to undergo a painful operation in order to touch the hearts of the pitiful. Sometimes they accomplish the same end by artifice, just as the London beggars do."

"You mean that they pretend to have something dreadful the matter with them when they really haven't?"

"Yes. I will tell you one such case. A poor man came to a missionary at Ningpo one day with his wrist bandaged up. He said that he had fallen into the hands of the pirates, who had hacked it almost off. His story excited the compassion of the missionary; but instead of giving him some money, as doubtless the man hoped he would, the missionary thought he could give him more permanent assistance. He called a sedan chair, and placing the sufferer in it, hurried him off to the missionary hospital. When the surgeon heard the story he announced that it was an undoubted case for amputation, and proceeded most tenderly to remove the bandages. The man groaned when the wounded limb was touched, and seemed to be suffering great torture. Bandage after bandage was taken off, and when the wrist was at last reached, it was found to be perfectly sound."

"That is just like some of the beggars in England, is not it?" said Mabel. "Some of the people who look so miserable in the London streets, and make you feel so sorry for them as you pass them, are cheats like that, are not they? and their lame legs and powerless arms become just like other people's when they get into their nightly dens."

"I expect that the race of beggars are very much the same all the world over," said Mrs. Foster. "But there are some things about the beggars of China which are quite peculiar. A great many of them are regularly organized into companies, with a head man or king over them. This man is elected on account of his talents in the art of begging, and all the spoils gathered by the different members of the company are given up to him, and he dispenses to them food and clothing. One of his principal duties is to levy a tax upon the chief shops of the city in which he and his subjects may chance to live. He makes up his mind what sum the master of each establishment ought to contribute, and then goes and haggles with him, and bullies him, until the unfortunate man consents to the payment. That done, his majesty gives the shopman two papers, one green and one red. On them is written the king's name, the sum of money agreed upon, and the days when it is paid, and then is added, 'The brethren must not come here to molest and annoy.' If after this any one of the club should venture to be troublesome, the shopman is at perfect liberty to beat him. In this way alone the beggars make no inconsiderable revenue. There is, I believe, one grocer's shop in Ningpo which is said to contribute somewhere about £140 per annum to these headmen."

"But what happens," inquired Frank, "if the shopman says he will give nothing? Surely the beggars cannot make him."

"Indeed, they can. A troop of them assault his house, and make themselves so supremely disagreeable that he is only too glad to pay a sum even larger than that he refused before, in order to be rid of the nuisance."

"But it seems such a strange thing that such conduct should be allowed," said Mabel. "I should have thought that the Government would have put an end to it."

"But, you see, it does not," replied Mrs. Foster. "The beggars in China seem, in fact, to be quite a recognized class, and to have their rights, like any other order in the empire. It is considered their privilege, for instance, to bury criminals after an execution, and they are paid a regular fee for the job. Private persons also make use of them. If a creditor gets tired of waiting for payment, it is no uncommon plan for him to give his bill to a band of beggars, and making them promise to let him have part of the spoil, to set them on the unfortunate debtor. They go and worry him day by day, until at last, if it is anyhow within the bounds of possibility, he produces the money, just to escape from the torment.

"Then, too, on all important occasions, such as marriages or funerals, the beggars are sure to appear, and cannot be got rid of until money has been given to them. On the occasion of a wedding, indeed, they generally pay more than one visit. On the day of the event itself they chant all manner of good wishes to the happy pair, and are duly paid with money. Then the next day they make their appearance again, demanding the remains of the feast. At funerals, they often will not allow the solemn rites to proceed until a large sum has been given to them. Indeed, I have read of one case in which they demanded a sum equivalent to £4, and one of their number got into the grave, and positively refused to allow the coffin to be lowered, hoping by this means to extort the enormous sum which they demanded. However, after waiting for a considerable period, and finding the mourners hard to tire out, they at last consented to accept three shillings.

"There is one class of beggars who look upon themselves, and, I suppose, are looked upon by the people, as protectors against evil spirits. At the annual feast to the beggar-ghosts they always claim the remains. As a class, these beggars have the character of being thieves, though, from the name by which they are called, namely, 'the high-flower people,' one would imagine that they have a very high opinion of themselves. The story of their origin is just this:—Tsaou-wâng, a man who is supposed to have lived about 1,000 years ago, had nearly obtained the highest degree at the central examination, when some malicious evil spirits got hold of him, and so scratched and disfigured his face, that the emperor refused to grant it. Of course, the poor man was wofully disappointed, and the emperor, to comfort him, gave him a knife three feet long, with which he was to extirpate all evil spirits. I do not know whether the 'high-flower people' are descendants of his; but, at any rate, they claim to rule over the evil spirits, and, whenever possible, to extirpate them in his name. Each house gives to three, but not more than three, of these protectors.

"At Ningpo there is a kind of asylum for diseased

and deformed beggars. The way to get admitted to this asylum is to give a sumptuous feast to the inmates. The emperor allows each beggar in the asylum eight or nine dollars annually, and those that are able go out and beg daily, probably exciting a great deal of pity by their wretched appearance.

"But there are some beggars that are lower down in the scale of humanity than any of those I have told you about. They are beggars who have, at one time, been criminals, and they generally carry the badges of their crime about with them. Sometimes one of them may be seen with a wooden collar around his neck, which is a model of the heavy one borne by convicted thieves; or you may meet another with a spear padlocked to his foot and shoulder."

"Do not the Chinese have some very horrible punishments?" inquired Tom.

"Yes; I think they are tolerably ingenious in inventing horrible torture. That of the wooden collar, or the punishment of the 'Tcha,' as it is called, is a very common one for small offences. It consists of an immense piece of wood, with a hole for the head and another for the hands. Sometimes a man is condemned to wear it for several months. He may stand up or move about as much as his chain will allow; but gene-

PUNISHMENT OF THE TCHA.

rally the weight of the collar is so great that he finds it hard to rise."

"But what do you mean by the chain, mamma?" said Mabel. "What is the man chained to?"

"To some wall in the public thoroughfare, in order that the disgrace may be made thoroughly public, and that others may be deterred from committing like offences. Of course, any one who is condemned to this very uncomfortable kind of adornment is rendered perfectly helpless, and sometimes the relations of the culprits may be seen feeding them, or washing their faces for them."

"It must be something like the stocks that people used to be put into in England, mustn't it," said Grace, "only far more uncomfortable? I should think it must be rather an effectual kind of punishment. But tell us, mamma, what other things they do to people that have done wrong?"

"For great crimes people are put to death, generally being strangled. That mode of death is considered much less disgraceful than having the head cut off; but sometimes, I suppose, in cases where the offence has been very great, people are beheaded, and the head is stuck up in some conspicuous place, as a warning to others. Horrible stories are told of these heads being sometimes carried off by beggars, salted, and eaten; but I should hope such stories are not true.

"One of the commonest and mildest forms of punishment is flogging with the split bamboo. This is inflicted for very small offences. The culprit is made to lie flat on the ground, and receive, perhaps, thirty stripes.

"Torture is, I believe, sometimes inflicted in order to extort confessions from those who are suspected of crimes, but how often this is the case I cannot ascertain. Travellers differ in their opinions. Some speak of it as frequently used, and others seem to consider it as of rare occurrence. One instrument of torture is a kind of cage, the upper part of which is composed of two planks furnished with spikes, which can be brought together so as to enclose a man's neck without allowing him to slip his head through. The planks are then raised to such a height as will enable the man to escape hanging if he stands on the tips of his toes. Another method of torture is to hang a man by one hand and one foot. Then the Chinese have pincers for tearing out the nails and eyes; curry-combs with razor blades for scraping and cutting the skin, and other horrible things which it makes one shudder to think of."

"These are very much like the things that the Roman Catholics used to have in the Inquisition, are not they?" said Mabel. "But won't you tell us something more about the beggars, mamma? Do the Chinese do anything to help them besides giving them money? I mean, have they any institutions, such as there are in England, for making the people better? Do they try to make them leave off being beggars?"

"I fear not, Mabel. Such a thing is scarcely to be expected of a heathen nation. More, perhaps, is done for the relief of the wretched creatures than might have been looked for. At one time the Government in Pekin erected some small houses for the shelter of beggars during the cold nights of winter. These houses were called 'Feather-houses,' because they were furnished with a quantity of feathers, in which the poor wretches nestled. Then, I believe, in some part of China, there is, or was, an institution where one enormous coverlet is let down at night upon a crowd of beggars who creep under it for shelter. Private people, too, will sometimes give away food and clothing on a large scale. In the winter of 1832, which was a very cold and rainy one, a lady in Canton gave away 1,500 jackets to the old and infirm beggars of the city."

"Do you think the beggars are very wretched, really?" inquired Frank. "Don't you think they have jolly times when they are out of sight, and keep all their wretchedness for the public gaze?"

"No doubt there are a great many impostors among them, as is the case with the beggars in every land; and, probably, the majority have such a love for a vagrant life that there could be little hope of making them anything better. There is a Chinese proverb, 'Three years a beggar, who would be a king?' But, in spite of that, there are sights to be seen in China which render it impossible to believe that there is not a fearful amount of suffering and misery among them. I read an account the other day of a place in the suburbs of Canton called the Beggars' Square, which will, I think, convince you of this. It is a large open space, about a hundred yards square. On one side there are a number of temples, and in the adjacent streets there are some very respectable-looking houses. There are, too, a great many apothecaries' shops, the outsides of which are covered with a number of old rags."

"Whatever are they?" said Tom.

"They are plasters which have been used with great success by the apothecary's patients, and which he, therefore, nails up in full view of all the passers-by, in order that they may see what a singularly clever man he is. Well, these are the surroundings of the square.

In the centre may be seen idle vagabonds, gambling or amusing themselves in other vicious ways, and, side by side with them, a number of poor emaciated creatures lying on mats, some dying, some already dead. The missionary who gives the account, struck with the horror of the scene, and anxious to assure himself of the truth of the case, lifted the mat from some of those who were quite motionless, and thus proved that there were, at least, four corpses in the horrible assembly."

"And the priests close by let the people die without doing anything to help them?" said Grace; "for, I suppose, there were priests in the temples. But do the Christian missionaries do anything for the beggars, mamma?"

"I do not know of any particular work of theirs among the beggars; though, no doubt, they do what they can amongst them. But beggars are always a very difficult class of people to deal with anywhere, and especially among a heathen nation. It is so difficult to tell whether they are sincere when they express an interest in what is told them, and whether they are not professing what they do not feel, merely in the hopes of pleasing you, and consequently getting something out of you."

CHAPTER VI.

OPIUM AND TEA.

"WON'T you tell us a little about the opium-eaters of China to-day, Mrs. Foster?" said Frank Mason, at the next meeting of the little workers. "You were telling us about the beggars last time, and I suppose it is opium-smoking which makes a great many people beggars, isn't it, just as drinking does in England?"

"I have no doubt that is the case. If it is possible, opium-smoking is a vice which gets even a tighter hold upon a man than drinking does, and is most deadly in its effects. Many drunkards live to be old men, but an opium-smoker very rarely does. The struggle, too, to break loose from the habit is most fearful. I will give an account of a victim to the vice, who once came to a missionary to beg for a cure. He was a shoemaker by trade, and about thirty-seven years old. His face was fearfully bloated, and he looked exceedingly weak and ill. He told the missionary that he had smoked opium for about thirteen years, but was most anxious to reform, asking him if he could not tell him of some medicine that would enable him to do so. It was pitiable to hear the manner in which he described the fatal chains that the vice had cast around him. He said he fainted at his work if he did not take his accustomed quantity, and could not retain his food. At the same time, while the drug gave a little temporary strength, it gradually produced fearful weakness, and destroyed all hearty appetite. It also was ruinous to his pocket, taking each day the lion's share of his wages. He implored the missionary to tell him of some means whereby he might be cured; and when the latter directed him to pray for divine grace, he said that he had worshipped Shangti on the birthday of the idol with that intention. The poor fellow seemed so thoroughly in earnest that the missionary asked him whether he would like to go with him to his own house for a few days, as there he would be out of the way of temptation. The offer was most gratefully accepted, and accordingly he presented himself the next morning. For a few hours he behaved very well, but as evening drew on became very restless and uncomfortable. He began to talk with the missionary, and it was evident that a bitter struggle was going on within. The craving, no doubt, was insupportable to unassisted human nature; and he invented a pretext for going out, but, as he had no money, that was of no use. Then he apparently suddenly bethought of his family, and said that, as he was not at home, they would have no money to buy rice. The missionary knew only too well what this meant, and therefore firmly refused to produce the little cash that the man begged for. The man remained in the missionary's house a short time longer, evidently in a state of the most acute suffering, and then suddenly disappeared into the street."

"But what makes people begin to smoke in the first instance?" said Tom. "I should have thought, when they saw people around them made wretched by it, they would have a perfect horror of it."

"One would think the same of drunkenness," said Mrs. Foster; "that the wretchedness it produces would be quite enough to deter people from drinking to excess. But we know well enough it does not. People get drawn into it by degrees. And it is just the same with opium. Perhaps a man is not quite well, and a friend says to him, 'Try a little opium. It would do you good.' And he does try it, and finds it does relieve his pain, and produces a very pleasant sensation. So the next time he is a little indisposed he tries it again, and then by-and-by he smokes a pipe when he has no pain; and so he goes down the hill until he becomes a confirmed opium-smoker. Or another way in which a man falls a prey to the vice is this: he is asked by a friend to go with him to an opium-house; he feels some reluctance, but does not like to say no, and therefore goes. At first he does not smoke, but it is always unpleasant to be peculiar, so in a little while he takes a pipe. He finds it far more agreeable than he expected, and therefore the next time feels no reluctance when invited. In a very short time no invitation at all is needed; he is a regular attendant at the house, and opium has become a necessary of his existence."

"But are there regular places for smoking in?" inquired Frank. "I should have thought people would have done it in their own houses."

"The richer people, I fancy, do; but the poorer ones frequent the opium-shops, and smoke there, just in the same way as poor people in England drink in the public-houses."

"What sort of places are the opium-houses?" inquired one of the children.

"The missionary whom I mentioned just now describes one of the opium-houses that he visited.

He says it had four or five rooms opening upon a square court, and in each of these rooms lay men stretched upon couches, having at their heads a lamp, pipes, and all the apparatus for smoking. In the centre stood the master of the establishment, weighing out the prepared drug, while several men were lounging about looking with envious eyes at the smokers, and wishing that they had money enough to enjoy the like luxury."

"Haven't the English had a good deal to do with making the Chinese so devoted to opium?"

"I am sorry to say that we have. The conduct of England in the matter has been very dreadful, and will long, I fear, be a great hindrance to mission work. The Chinese Emperor was anxious to prevent opium being brought into the country, knowing, I suppose, the fatal liking which his people have for it, and how destructive it is in its effects. But large quantities of it are grown in the British possessions in India, and China is a most convenient market for it, so we have forced it upon them with our guns."

"You mean there have been wars about it, mamma?"

"Yes; and unhappily the Chinese cannot forget our conduct in the matter, and therefore are not prepossessed in favour of missionaries who come from a country that has done their land so much harm. In fact, the missionary whom I spoke of just now was at once reproved when he reasoned with the opium-smokers, for they asked him how the English could be so inconsistent as to argue against a habit which their own ships brought the poor Chinese the means of indulging. Several of the men to whom he spoke expressed the greatest astonishment when they heard he was an Englishman, and said that they thought all missionaries came from America, and all opium people from England. The ship in which this missionary went to China contained a considerable quantity of opium, and a Chinese boy whom he had with him on board asked him what he would say to the Chinese if, after hearing him talk about the Lord Jesus Christ, they should inquire why he had come in a ship which brought so much poison to their country. I do not know what the missionary replied, but you see what a stumbling-block this opium-trade is."

"Still, after all, mamma," said Tom, "it is very much the Chinese's own fault. They are not forced to buy it—they are quite free to refuse it; and if they did, the English people would soon give up taking it there. But what does it look like? Is it simply the poppy-heads that the people sell, or is the opium extracted and prepared?"

"The missionary whom I mentioned just now describes some which he saw as being made up into balls and packed in boxes; he says that each box contained about forty of these balls, all placed in separate partitions, and that the box was worth about £200. When a Chinese merchant meditated purchasing from a ship, a little piece would be broken off some of these balls and carefully tested to see whether it was pure. And the English traders were equally careful in the examination of the silver which they received in payment. He says it was painful to him to see the earnestness of all the persons concerned in the wretched trade. It is not easy to excite a Chinese to anything like enthusiasm or eagerness, but opium seems to do it when other higher matters entirely fail."

"But, after all, Mrs. Foster," said Frank, "I suppose it is only a very small proportion of the Chinese who smoke opium. I do not mean to say that it is not very dreadful that even so many should do it as do. But I suppose it is very much the same with opium-smoking as it is with drinking. Sometimes you hear people talk as if nearly all the people of England were drunkards, and yet I am sure they are not. And, just in the same way, no doubt in China there are heaps of people who never think of taking opium at all."

"The population of China is so very great that it would be sad indeed if there were not, as you say, heaps of people who have nothing to do with opium; but, at the same time, the proportion of habitual smokers is very dreadful. It is, I believe, very nearly half; and as the habit, you see, ruins a man's health, and almost invariably shortens his life, I should fear that the population of China will rapidly decrease under the influence of the curse."

"That seems a pity, doesn't it?" said Mabel. "I think it is always rather sad to hear of the population of a place becoming smaller, and I never can bear to think of how the people of Australia, and the New Zealanders, are dying out; but it seems much worse if an old people like the Chinese begin to go down—a people, too, that are so clever, and have so long been civilized. Did Sophy show you, mamma, that book, the other day, that she had full of Chinese pictures? Some of them were so very good, there was so much expression on some of the people's faces, and so much spirit in the pictures, only it is such a pity that they do not understand perspective. They always draw everything going up such a very steep hill. I can't think how it is that they don't see it is wrong."

"It does seem curious," said Mrs. Foster, "and it is not only their perspective that is in fault, but their light and shade. And the funny thing is that a picture well drawn, with due regard to these important particulars, strikes them as unnatural and incorrect. Some portraits executed by first-rate European artists were once sent as a present to the Chinese Emperor, and the light and shade in the pictures at once struck some mandarins, to whom they were shown, as a serious imperfection. One man asked whether the people whose portraits they were had the two sides of their faces of different colours. The shadow cast by the nose they considered a great blemish to the picture, and some of them thought it had got there by mistake. An Italian missionary, who was an excellent painter, was once commissioned by the Emperor to paint him several pictures, but he was told that he must do them in the Chinese style, not in the European. I do not know how he liked his job, but he produced some pictures exceedingly well done, as far as regarded form and colour, but utterly ineffective owing to the want of shadow. However, the Emperor was far better pleased than he would have been with any productions wrought with proper regard to perspective, and light and shade."

BRONZE LION.

"But do not the Chinese see that things in reality do not look the same on the two sides?" said Mabel.

"Surely they must, and they must see, too, that things look smaller the further they are away from us."

"Yes, I think they do see both those things," replied Mrs. Foster. "But they consider shade is a merely accidental circumstance in nature—in fact, I suppose, a kind of mistake, as it dims the brightness of the colouring; and they think that it certainly ought not to be repeated on canvas. In the same way, they look upon the apparently diminished size of objects at a distance as arising from an imperfection in our sight, and think it right, therefore, to represent things as they know they are, not as they appear. It is a wonderful theory, no doubt, but one which completely prevents any Chinese artist rising to anything like excellence. The point in which they do excel is brilliancy of colouring. They draw, too, with great accuracy, and their representations of animals are generally very good. But they cannot group figures together at all well, and therefore their pictures are always ineffective."

"Do they make good statues?" said Mabel. "Perspective would not be necessary for them, or any knowledge of light and shade."

"Quite true, still their statues are not good. They appear to have an aversion to the science of anatomy, and therefore, of course, cannot excel. Here is a picture of a Chinese statue of a lion, which you will at once see needs to have written under it, 'This is a lion.'"

"Most undoubtedly it does," replied Tom, "and a good deal of faith is necessary to believe it even then. Why, the creature looks as if it had got a lawyer's wig on, with an extra big bow at the bottom. Is there anything peculiar about the lions in China, or do you think the sculptor had never seen one?"

"I should think that that is most probable, for the lion is not a native of China, and I do not suppose has ever been brought into the country, either as a present to the Emperor, or as a show for the people; for I don't think they have menageries or zoological gardens, as we do. Probably the sculptor had only read about the lion, or, perhaps, seen a bad picture of him, and made the figure very much out of his own head. He knew it was very fierce, and therefore made the teeth very conspicuous, but certainly succeeded in representing a most ill-tempered looking beast, and one very different from the noble animal you and I know the lion to be."

"Are there any elephants in China?" said Frank; "or is it too far north for them?"

"There are no elephants that are native to the country, but a good many are brought from countries further south. Indeed, the animal is a good deal used, and much valued. It becomes quite granivorous, being fed almost entirely on rice, instead of eating the tender shoots of young trees as it does in its wild state."

"What a queer idea!" said Tom; "I hope they are fonder of it than I am. I would not do much work for people who kept me upon rice-pudding, I know that. But I suppose they don't take the trouble to boil it for the elephants; the creatures have to eat it dry. I hope they have satisfactory teeth, for rice always wants such an amount of chewing. And I should think they give them tea to drink, don't they? Everybody and everything drinks tea in China, doesn't it?"

"Everybody, perhaps," said Mrs. Foster, "but not everything. It is too precious to be wasted upon animals; for, though so largely cultivated in the country, there is a ready sale for it in other parts of the world; and the quantity yearly exported is enormous. It is grown principally upon the slopes of the hills, and flourishes best in those provinces that border upon the sea coast."

"What does the tea grow like?" inquired one of the children. "Is it a little plant, or does it grow upon trees?"

"The tea-plant is a shrub, and it bears a little white flower. It is the leaves of this shrub that we make into a drink, but they are first properly prepared, being dried upon a hot plate. They are also most carefully sorted, and in fact go through a great many processes before they are finally packed into chests and sent to England."

"But they don't all come to England, do they?" inquired one little girl, looking astonished. "I suppose the Chinese send it to other countries, as well as to England, don't they?"

"You are quite right," said Mrs. Foster. "They do send it to other countries as well as to England, but we, I fancy, get far the most of it. You see we English people are so fond of a comfortable cup of tea that everybody drinks it who can anyhow get it. But in France or Spain, people very much prefer coffee, and do not drink it much, except they are ill."

"Do the Chinese drink it as we do—with milk and sugar?" said Frank.

"No," replied Mrs. Foster, "that they would consider a great mistake; and they do not use a teapot either. They just put a few tea-leaves into a cup and pour some boiling water upon them. They then cover the cup up for a few minutes, until the tea is ready. It seems to me a bungling way of doing it, and I think that our teapots are much better, because the strainer, if it is a good one, keeps the leaves from going into the cup at all."

"Don't the Chinese have kind of public tea-houses, just as in England we have public-houses where the people sell beer and spirits?"

"Yes," replied Mrs. Foster, "and much better kind of public-houses they are. There is generally a large room, with a number of little tables set out in it, just as in an English coffee-room: and if you go and sit down at one of these tables, some tea is at once brought to you, together with cakes and tarts and sweetmeats, for the Chinese are first rate at confectionery."

"I suppose tea is the principal thing that the Chinese export, isn't it?" said Mabel. "They certainly give us a very much more useful thing than we give them. I wouldn't exchange tea for opium if I were they."

"Opium," said Mrs. Foster, "like all the things which God has made, has its use. In certain cases of illness, it is a most invaluable medicine, and the mistake which the Chinese make is in using it wrongly. They in fact abuse God's good gift, instead of using it. But you are right in imagining that tea is the principal export of China. As I told you just now, we are the largest customers for it. A great deal goes to the United States, and Russia and Holland also import a great deal. But none of the other nations of Europe care much about it."

"I always think that seems so funny," said Mabel; "and I never can make out how people got on before tea was introduced into England. Whatever did all the old women do? They always seem almost to live on tea now. Why, the old women in the almshouses often have tea three times a day, I know."

"And yet people used to have to do without it," said Mrs. Foster, "for it was not introduced at all into this country until the seventeenth century. The first mention of it is an act of Parliament in 1660, by which we find that a duty of eighteenpence a gallon was charged upon it when sold in the public-houses. Pepys, too, a writer who lived at that time, and whose diary you will be interested some day in reading, says, 'Sept. 25th, I sent for a cup of tea (a Chinese drink) of which I had never drank before.'"

"But how queer it must have been to buy it in that way!" said Grace. "I suppose it was sold cold like beer. I wonder whether people drank it in that way, or whether they warmed it up. Even if they did, it must have been rather horrid, for I think there is nothing much nastier than stale tea. Even poor people now don't much care about it. Cook was saying, only the other day, that nobody cared to take the trouble to fetch it. But of course it was much more expensive when people first began to use it than it is now."

"Rather!" said Mrs. Foster. "In 1664 a present of two pounds two ounces was made to Charles II. by the East India Company, and what do you think was the price of it then? Try and guess."

"Fifteen or sixteen shillings?" said Tom.

"Far more than that. It was at that time about two guineas a pound, so you can imagine almshouse old women had to do without it then. Indeed that two pounds two ounces was probably all the tea there was in London, and they most likely were procured from the continent; for the East India Company did not make its first regular importation till 1669, when they brought in two canisters containing 150 pounds."

"How absurd that sounds!" said Frank. "A hundred and fifty pounds! Why, one grocer's shop would get rid of that in no time now. How much tea do we get from China now, mamma? Have you any idea?"

"I am afraid I could not tell you at all exactly; but I believe in the year 1869 England paid to China for tea somewhere about £5,000,000, and no doubt the sum goes on increasing every year."

"What an enormous lot of money!" said Frank. "The Chinese must be rather glad that they at last made up their minds to open their ports to us; don't you think they must, Mrs. Foster?"

"Certainly. And we have cause to be glad too; for if we buy from them, they also buy from us. The English plenipotentiary who signed the treaty in 1842 said that he was opening to the trade of England a country so vast that all the looms of Lancashire would not suffice to clothe one of its provinces. And so it has proved, for the imports are even larger than the exports, and the amount of cotton cloth sent into China is enormous."

"Does not the tea-plant look rather like a camellia?" inquired a little girl who seldom spoke; "I heard a gentleman who came from China tell papa the other day that some tea is made from the leaves of camellias, but he said that the Chinese ought not to do it, for it was cheating. He said that there was one kind of camellia that made very good tea indeed, and that the tea-plant is really a kind of camellia, only he said the Chinese very often used wrong kinds."

"Very likely," replied Mrs. Foster; "I am afraid the habit of cheating and adulteration is pretty general. But no doubt this gentleman talked about the way in which the tea is prepared. See if you cannot give us the benefit of the conversation."

Poor Lucy blushed, and looked rather alarmed; but, like a wise child, she made up her mind to do her best, though she inwardly wished she had not spoken.

"Mr. Jay did tell us about it," she began, "but I am afraid I shan't remember it all properly. I muddle up things so. I know he said the leaves are all dried on iron plates, just as you told us, Mrs. Foster. He said it is done in little houses where there are a number of small furnaces about three feet high. He said the plates are put on the top of these furnaces. There is a long table in the building, and on this table some people roll out the leaves, and then, when the plates are hot, they put them on the pan and keep on moving them about until they get too hot to touch. The heat of the iron makes them crack, and when they are very hot indeed they take them off the plate with a kind of shovel like a fan, and put them on to some mats.

Then some other people take small quantities of them in the palms of their hands, and roll them, I think to make them curl up nicely; and while they do that some other people fan them to make them cool quickly. I think Mr. Jay said that was all that was done, only he said it was done two or three times over, in order to make sure that the tea was quite dry, and that each time the plate was cooler than it was the time before, and the whole thing was done more slowly and carefully. Of course the tea had to be sorted after this, and Mr. Jay said that the different kinds of tea did not only depend upon its coming from different places, or even upon the leaves being of different ages, but he said the tea is winnowed, and the heaviest is considered the best. He said that is what people call gunpowder tea, and that the light tea is the worst. Another thing Mr. Jay said too, and that is that the tea got from Russia is the best, and he said that for a long time people thought it was because the Russians brought it from China overland, and that a sea voyage wasn't good for tea, but that the real reason is that the Russians get it from a different part, where the soil is better and the plant grows finer. I think that was all Mr. Jay said. At least I can't remember anything else."

"Well, you have given us a very nice account," said

Mrs. Foster. And Mabel added, " I am sure I shouldn't have told it half as well. I always begin at the wrong end, if I try to tell anything, or else leave out some of the most important particulars. But, mamma," she added, " don't the Chinese send us a great deal of silk too ? "

" Yes, my dear; silk has always been one of the most important exports of China. Indeed, until the time of the Emperor Justinian, the silkworm was, I believe, only cultivated in that country. It feeds, you know, upon mulberry leaves, and there are great numbers of mulberry trees in China."

"But silkworms will live upon other things," said Grace. " Don't you remember, mamma, some we had two or three years ago? We used to feed them upon lettuce leaves. And we got a good deal of silk from them too. Mabel has quite a good-sized skein of it somewhere. Have not you, Mabel ? "

" I know silkworms will eat lettuce leaves," replied Mrs. Foster, "but they do not thrive upon them. Mulberry leaves is their natural food, and it is of no use to give them anything else if you have them for use, not merely for amusement. How far do you think your skein would go, Grace, towards making silk for a dress ? and how many cocoons do you think are necessary to produce an ounce of silk."

"I am sure I do not know, mamma. As many as 30 or 40?"

"Put another 0 to your thirty, and then you will not be far from the mark. So you see it is no wonder that silk is not a very cheap material, and that it is quite necessary to feed the worms on the food which best suits them if you mean to make much money by the cultivation of silk. It was the Chinese who first discovered its use, and their most ancient records describe the queen and her attendants as engaged in the silk manufacture. Indeed it seems to have been known to them somewhere about 2000 B.C."

"They seem to me to have found out everything almost as soon as ever they could," exclaimed Tom. "Why, the Flood was not so very long before that, was it? What a pity it seems that they did not go on and improve and make fresh discoveries as people do now. Why, what numbers of discoveries have been made in the last hundred years! If the Chinese had gone on at the same rate ever since they began to find out things, what a heap they would know by this time! But I say, mamma, are mulberries very cheap there?— because I suppose the silkworms don't eat the fruit, only the leaves."

"The mulberries that are cultivated for the silkworms do not produce much fruit. It is the leaves that are wanted, and the trees are continually pruned, in order to make them produce a constant succession of young shoots, these young shoots being the best food for the worms. The trees are grown in regular plantations, and the worms are reared for the most part in houses built for the purpose in the plantations. They are supposed to prosper better here than in town; any noise, even the barking of a dog, being considered bad for them. The worms are always suffocated before the silk is wound off, and when freed from their covering are cooked and served up to table as a nice dish."

"Very nice indeed, I should think!" said Mabel. "To think of eating worms! How can any one do it?"

PEKIN.

CHAPTER VII.

PEKIN, NANKIN, AND CANTON.

"I THINK, to-day," said Mrs. Foster, "I had better tell you something about some of the cities of China, and I will begin with its capital. I wonder whether any one can tell me what it is."

No one spoke for some minutes; every one, I suppose, being afraid of making a mistake, but at length Mabel said,—

"I know that Pekin, Nankin, and Canton are the three principal cities, but I really don't know which is considered its capital."

"It is Pekin," said Mrs. Foster, smiling, "which I hope, at any rate, you all remember is in the north of China. It is an inland city, and is surrounded by very high walls. The principal palace of the Emperor is situated in it, and the streets are wide and well built. It at once, however, strikes a European as very singular in its appearance, from the fact that few of the houses are more than one story high, none more than two."

"The houses must be very small then, aren't they?" said Tom; "or else they must take up an immense lot of room. Only fancy if the houses in London were all low like that! Why, I should think it would take up three or four counties, and I am sure it is big enough as it is. But I suppose Pekin has not such a number of people living in it as London, has it?"

"It is difficult to discover what is its population, accounts differ so much. Some people say 1,500,000, some 2,000,000, some 3,000,000, and, according to the calculation that was made in the last century by a Jesuit called Grimaldi, it was then 16,000,000. But that seems perfectly incredible, and I should be disposed to take the lowest figures, as most likely to be correct. At first sight it is, I believe, difficult to credit that even that number can be contained in the place, but the fact is a Chinese family does not require so much room as an English one. They do not mind being in rather close quarters. The families, you know, are much larger than with us; for when a man marries he does not set up a house of his own, but brings his wife into his father's house, so that what we should consider a number of families live under one roof. There may, perhaps, be an old man and his wife, then, say, four or five sons and their wives and children, and perhaps half a dozen grandsons and their wives and children."

"How queer that must seem!" said Mabel; "but it is just the same in India, isn't it? I don't think I should like it at all, it can't be half so snug as our way of living. But, mamma, for such mobs of people the houses must surely be very big."

"Of course all the families are not as large as the one I have imagined. But, as I told you, the Chinese don't mind a bit of a squeeze. Each branch of the family only needs one sleeping room, the beds being divided by mats hung from the ceiling, and the whole party feed in one common room."

Well, I am glad I don't live in China, or Pekin, at any rate," said Frank. "But how big is the city, Mrs. Foster?"

"The city itself covers fourteen square miles, and then it has extensive suburbs, so that it is difficult to form a distinct idea of its whole size. Of course, as you know, the suburbs of London are much larger than the city, and possibly it may be the same at Pekin. The city is built so as to form an exact square, and is divided into two, the one inhabited by Chinese and the other by Tartars. The wall which surrounds the Tartar city is very high indeed, and so broad that twelve horsemen could easily ride abreast; and at intervals there are large towers big enough to contain good large bodies of soldiers."

"How fond the Chinese seem to be of walls!" said Tom. "What a labour it must have been to make such a wall!"

"Not quite the same labour as the Great Wall, though," said Mrs. Foster. "A people that could accomplish that could never be daunted by anything, I should think. But I must go on to tell you more about Pekin. The city has nine gates, all lofty, and well arched. Over them there are towers nine stories high, each story having a good many port-holes in it. The lowest story forms a large hall for the use of the soldiers quitting and relieving guard. Most of the streets of Pekin are straight, and the principal ones broad and long, and bordered with shops. These shops are generally gaily painted, and often along the tops run broad terraces decorated with flowers and shrubs."

"How pretty they must look!" said Grace; "and are the streets full?"

"Yes, the number of people that throng them is wonderful; and the confusion of horses, camels, mules, and carriages is as great as that in the crowded parts of London; but one thing must make them look very singular, and that is the absence of women, whose small feet prevent them going abroad.

"The Emperor's principal palace is in Pekin, in the Tartar city, and a most wonderful place it is. It is not one great building, but a perfect assemblage of vast buildings, immense courts, and magnificent gardens. The ground of the city generally is flat, Pekin standing on a plain, but the ground enclosed by the palace wall is much diversified, artificial hills having been formed, and the hollows caused by their formation having been turned into pretty lakes, on the largest of which there are a number of small islands. On the tops of the hills there are groups of trees, and, in many cases, delightful summer-houses. In one of these the Emperor who first of all constructed the palace and laid out the grounds came to a sad end. He had been a languid, indolent sort of governor, more set upon his own comfort and pleasure than the good of his subjects; and, as is pretty sure to be the case in such circumstances, discontent arose. An army was drawn together, at first with the intention of frightening the Emperor into better behaviour. But, as often happens, this intention was soon lost sight of, and the leader of the army began to aim at the crown itself. He attacked the Emperor in his palace. The Emperor had not a sufficient force or enough energy to offer an effectual resistance; but he was determined not to fall into the hands of one of his subjects; he therefore first of all stabbed his only daughter, and then hanged himself."

"How dreadful!" said Grace. "I never can understand any one killing himself, whatever may be the matter. But the Chinese do not value life much, do they? They could not kill so many of their babies if they did."

"There seldom, if ever, is the same value for life among heathen nations as among those who have lived in the light of the gospel. And this is scarcely to be wondered at. The heathen do not know that self-murder is wrong, and they know nothing, certainly, of the life beyond the grave. It is therefore looked upon as a fine and spirited thing for a man to kill himself, rather than allow himself to fall into the hands of an enemy.

"However, I must go on. You will be amused, Tom, to hear that the wall round the palace enclosure is a double one, there being a considerable space between the two, which is occupied by tribunals, and by the horses belonging to the Emperor, and the officers of the court. One of the most remarkable things within the palace enclosure is the royal hall, called Taihotien. It is built upon a terrace, and has a great deal of white marble about it. It is about 130 feet long, and is almost square. The ceiling is carved and painted, and has a great many gilt dragons on it; but the walls are perfectly bare, having no ornament whatever either in the way of carving or pictures. The throne is in the centre, and has on it an inscription which means 'holy' or 'perfect.' To this throne, as well as to the image of the Emperor, the Chinese offer something very like divine honours. The Emperor himself never appears in public without 2,000 lictors bearing axes. Yet, in spite of this great state, the principle of the government is paternal. The Emperor looks upon himself, and is looked upon by others, as the father of his people, and he strives to make them feel himself their benefactor, and is jealous of any extensive acts of benevolence on the part of private persons. Thus, on one occasion, at a time of great distress, some merchants offered to spend a large sum upon the relief of a distressed province, but the

Emperor not only declined to allow the scheme to be carried out, but seemed almost offended that it should have been thought of."

"And do the people honour the Emperor very much?" inquired Grace.

"Yes, I think they do. As I told you some time ago, whatever else may be wrong or wanting in the Chinese character, the Chinaman understands and obeys the fifth commandment, and being, I suppose, from his cradle taught to look upon the Emperor as the father of his people, he feels for him very great reverence. This reverence shows itself in funny ways sometimes, as you shall hear. Towards the end of the last century a splendid carriage was sent by the English Government as a present to the Emperor. Nothing could be more admired, for though, I dare say, now we should think it a clumsy affair, it was vastly more comfortable than the Chinese vehicles. But one thing, it was pronounced, must be immediately altered. The coachman's box must be taken off. How any one could ever dream of placing any man's seat higher than that of the Emperor was perfectly inconceivable to the Chinese."

"Well!" said Frank, "the coachbox, I always say, is the best seat in a carriage; but I never thought of it as the place of honour. But what are the Chinese carriages like?"

"Very clumsy affairs indeed; in fact, little better than our carts. They have only two wheels, and are put straight on to the shafts without any springs at all, so that you can imagine they jolt considerably. Sedan chairs are a good deal used, such as you see in this picture. This is one which belonged to a person of great importance, and therefore is a good deal ornamented with tassels, &c. It is carried, you see, by four men, and four others accompany it to relieve the first bearers when they are tired."

"Used not people to go about in sedan chairs in England years ago?" said Frank.

"Yes, you may see one any day you like in the Kensington Museum; and it is a very few years indeed since they were entirely given up in Edinburgh. I remember very well going to a party in one when I was a girl. But I do not think the bearers would have undertaken to carry me again, for I remember I was so amused at my conveyance that I quite forgot it was necessary for the comfort of the men that I should sit still, and I jumped and danced about so, that they shrieked out to know whatever was the matter, and declared if I did not take care I should upset the thing.

That recalled me to my senses, and I remember I felt very small and uncomfortable when I arrived at my destination. I tried to get out with all the dignity befitting fifteen, but felt that the men must be thinking all the time what a child I was. But in China it is only the men who use sedan chairs. Ladies are carried about in close litters, which are slung between horses or mules.

"But I still have a little more to tell you about Pekin. It is in that city that the altars of heaven and earth have been constructed, at which the Emperor makes a solemn act of adoration once a year—at the altar of heaven when the sun is at the summer solstice, and at the altar of the earth in the winter. He is the only person that it is considered proper should worship at these altars, and there are grand processions on these occasions. The temple which contains the altar of heaven is of a circular form, because the sky as we gaze at it looks round, and it has the word 'tien,' or heaven, inscribed upon it. There is no image of any kind in the building. Neither is there any in the temple dedicated to the earth. That temple is square, because the ancients believed that to be the shape of the earth. Another annual ceremony, to which, no doubt, the juvenile Chinese look forward, is that of the Emperor

SEDAN CHAIR.

guiding the plough. In the spring he goes to the 'sien-nong-tan,' or eminence of agriculture, dressed like a farmer, all the nobles who surround him being in the same sort of attire. There he solemnly guides the plough for about half an hour, while peasants sing hymns in praise of agriculture. When he has had enough of it, the nobles take a turn, and each make a few furrows in the Emperor's presence. The fruit of this field is always kept most carefully separate from any other, and is solemnly pronounced the best in the land."

"What humbug!" said Tom, "as if it was in the least likely that the Emperor would plough better than those who were accustomed to such work. But what does he do it for?"

"It is meant as an encouragement to those engaged in farming," said Mrs. Foster; "and I dare say it has a good effect. But there is one thing more which I must not forget to tell you about Pekin. It is there, and there only, that the highest degrees of literature are conferred."

"You mean that it is there that the competitive examinations take place, don't you, mamma?" said Mabel. "Do tell us a little about them, because the others were not here when we were talking about them that day that we heard Jim had got in for the Civil Service. I did not know that all the examinations were held at Pekin. What a way it must be for some of the people to go!"

"It is not all the examinations that are held there," said Mrs. Foster, "only those for the higher degrees. You must know there are four degrees, the 'sew-tsai,' the 'keu-jin,' the 'tsin-sze,' and the 'han-tin.' The examination for the first, the 'sew-tsai' is conferred twice in every three years, in the principal city of each department, and of course a great many students never succeed in obtaining any higher degree. But people who have only that degree seldom get promoted to any political offices unless they have some private influence to back them. Even the keu-jin have generally to wait a good many years before they obtain any appointment. But the tsin-sze are sure of promotion at once. The examination for that degree only takes place once in three years, and it is only conferred on each occasion upon about 360 persons out of all the eighteen provinces of China. So you see it must be even a more difficult thing to obtain than an Indian Civil Service appointment, and no doubt there is an immense deal of rejoicing in a family when one of its number is successful. But the highest degree of all is very seldom obtained. The examination for that as well as for the tsin-sze takes place in Pekin, and it also is held once in three years. It is only conferred upon thirty persons each time, and the successful candidates are admitted to the National College, which forms a body of councillors to the Emperor, and from which the highest ministers of state are selected."

"But, mamma, there is one thing I want to ask you," said Mabel, "who are the mandarins? One always hears so much about them, and yet I never can make out very clearly who they are. Are they all the people who have obtained a degree?"

"No, they are taken from the literary class, but the majority of those who have passed the first and second examinations never become mandarins. They are the chief officers of the state, and are chosen by the Emperor. There is no hereditary aristocracy in China, at least none that has any influence. The Emperor supports his own relations, and allows them to wear narrow yellow girdles; but, unless any of them happen to be remarkably clever men, they seldom exercise any influence. The rank of the mandarins is shown by the colour of the buttons on their caps."

"Don't the Chinese wear a great many clothes?"

inquired Frank. "They always look as if they did in pictures."

"Very often they do. They put on one garment over another when it gets cold, instead of lighting a fire. Indeed, they have no fireplaces in their rooms, although, in the north of China, it is often very cold. They do, as you say, frequently look very much like bundles of clothes, and I am afraid they do not take their clothes off, either, quite as often as we should think desirable. They are not over fond of washing, and they do not undress at night as we do, but lie down in their clothes. In fact, they are a very dirty people altogether. As a rule, they dress in dark colours, but for mourning they wear white."

"How funny that seems!" said Grace. "Why, that is just the colour that we use at weddings. But I suppose they would not on any account wear it then."

"No, it is avoided, just in the same way as we avoid black. Bright colours are the proper thing at a wedding."

"Does that stuff called nankeen come from China?" inquired Lucy. "The name sounds something like Nankin."

"Yes," replied Mrs. Foster. "I cannot say whether all nankeen comes from Nankin now, but that is the place in which it was first made, and from which it took its name. There are large manufactories of it there now."

"Is Nankin as large a place as Pekin?" said Tom.

"I believe not," replied Mrs. Foster. "The population is reckoned as much smaller, and it seems to be a place that has very much declined both in size and importance. The space included within the walls is greater than that of any other town, but then a great part of it is in ruins, and a great deal of the ground is cultivated. It used, you know, to be the capital, and the name means southern court. King is the Chinese for court. Pekin means north court, and Nankin southern court. Nankin is now always called by the Chinese, in all official documents, Kiang-ning. It formerly had a magnificent palace, but not a vestige now remains. There still lingers a remembrance of temples, tombs of emperors, and other splendid monuments; but it is only a remembrance, the things themselves have passed away. Indeed, as far as buildings go, it is a thoroughly decayed place. Yet there is plenty of life in it too. The parts that are inhabited are exceedingly populous, and there is a great deal of business going on. It is the first city in China for manufactures. As I told you just now, a great deal of nankeen is made there, and there are also capital silk manufactories. It is famous, too, for its paper, and its printing, and its booksellers' shops. And it is a very learned city, and produces a great many doctors. But, I suppose, the most curious thing of all in it is its famous porcelain tower. Just try to imagine a building 200 feet high made of china. It is a pagoda of an octagonal shape, and is divided into nine stories, each story being finished off outside by projections of green tiles."

"I suppose, as far as shape goes, it is like that thing in the Kew Gardens, isn't it, mamma?" said Mabel.

"Yes, the pagoda at Kew is an imitation of the Chinese building. Of course pagodas are to be found in all parts of China, but this is, I believe, the only one that is made of china, and it is looked upon quite as one of the lions of Nankin. There is another nine-storied pagoda at Canton, but that is built in an ordinary way, and, apparently, is in a miserably ruinous condition. After the taking of Canton by the English in 1858, some of the conquering party wished to ascend it, but the staircase was in such a ruinous condition that the general forbade the attempt. There are three other pagodas in Canton, and all of them are built in honour of the dead."

PORCELAIN TOWER AT NANKIN.

"Oh, I thought pagodas were temples," said Tom.

"That is quite a mistake, though a very common idea," said Mrs. Foster. "The proper name for the buildings is Ta, and they have always been built either in memory of some dead person, or else just to make the landscape look pretty. A great many were built simply for this latter reason."

"Well, I never should have imagined that the Chinese would care much about that sort of thing," said Frank. "I should have thought that if they had any idea of beauty at all, they would not make such horrid frights of themselves. They generally have such very ugly faces, to begin with; and then they make them ten times worse by doing their hair in such a hideous fashion. But there is one thing I never can understand. They seem to shave off nearly all their hair, and yet, in pictures, their pigtails are often quite thick and long. How do they manage, mamma?"

"Much as the ladies of the present day do," replied Mrs. Foster. "If they have not enough hair of their own, they go to a shop and buy some. The greater part of a pigtail is often false. But I must tell you that if pigtails are not ornamental, they are often found very useful. They are splendid things, for instance, to catch a thief by, except, that is to say, in cases where they are entirely false; then, of course, they would simply come off in the hand. If people, too, are quarrelling, they present a most tempting means for a man to worry his antagonist by. You know Chinamen do not often come to a regular stand-up fight, as our John Bulls are rather too fond of doing; but if two Chinamen are quarrelling, you will often see them standing opposite to each other, making faces, and snarling like two cats. Then, suddenly, one of them will make a plunge at the other, and, seizing him by the pigtail, give him a good shake."

"Well, I should think it must make a fellow pretty helpless to be caught in that way," said Tom. "I don't quite see how he could defend himself; I should think there would be nothing for it but to kick up behind. But tell us something about Canton now, mamma. What sort of a place is it?"

"There is a good deal more that is interesting to tell you about Canton. It is built on the Se Kiang, and was for a long time the only city with which foreigners were allowed to trade. It is one of the oldest cities of China, or perhaps I should rather say there was a city, in very early times, on the same spot as that on which Canton now stands. The old city was burnt to ashes by the Tartars, and a new city has gradually risen upon its ruins. It is divided, like Pekin, into two parts, the Tartar and the Chinese city; but a large part of the population live entirely on the river. In fact, there are many people who have never spent a night on shore in their lives. A most curious appearance indeed the river must present. No more than a thin meandering line of water can be seen, so closely are the boats packed at the edge of each shore. Some people say that the dwellings of no less than 100,000 people are crowded together. Of course the majority of them are nothing more than things like the wretched little huts that one sees sometimes on the barges on the canals, but many of them are two-storied houses, and look perfectly firm and substantial. The town of Canton, you know, was bombarded and taken by the English a few years ago, and the flight of all this river population is described, by those who saw it, as a most singular sight. In a few hours the whole of this aquatic suburb disappeared, and houses that looked perfectly firmly established on the land were seen to unmoor themselves and scud off."

"But what makes the people live on the water in that way?" said Tom; "I don't see what they do it for."

"I really cannot tell you," said Mrs. Foster; "but I

believe the inhabitants of this floating city are forbidden by law to settle on land. You can imagine that it is not very pleasant to have to bring up a family in such quarters; the children not unfrequently tumble overboard, and no doubt make their mothers continually anxious. Not many little creatures, however, are, I believe, drowned, as it is customary to tie a hollow gourd round each child's neck, and this makes it float if it does tumble in. Besides, the river is so crowded that there are always plenty of people ready to pick any unfortunate little being up. It is not uncommon to make a garden on these floating rafts, and to rear vegetables. Two or three domestic animals, too, are not unfrequently kept."

"Well, it seems to me a most extraordinary idea to live in such very uncomfortable quarters, and if a great part of the ground within the walls has, as you said, no houses on it, I don't see the use of it. Why don't the people build houses there?"

"It was of Nankin that I said that was the case," replied Mrs. Foster; "I am afraid my story has not been interesting enough to keep you listening attentively. But it is equally true of Canton. Only about a third part of the ground is covered with buildings, the rest is taken up with pleasure-grounds and fishponds. These, however, I suppose belong to their respective owners who wish to keep them."

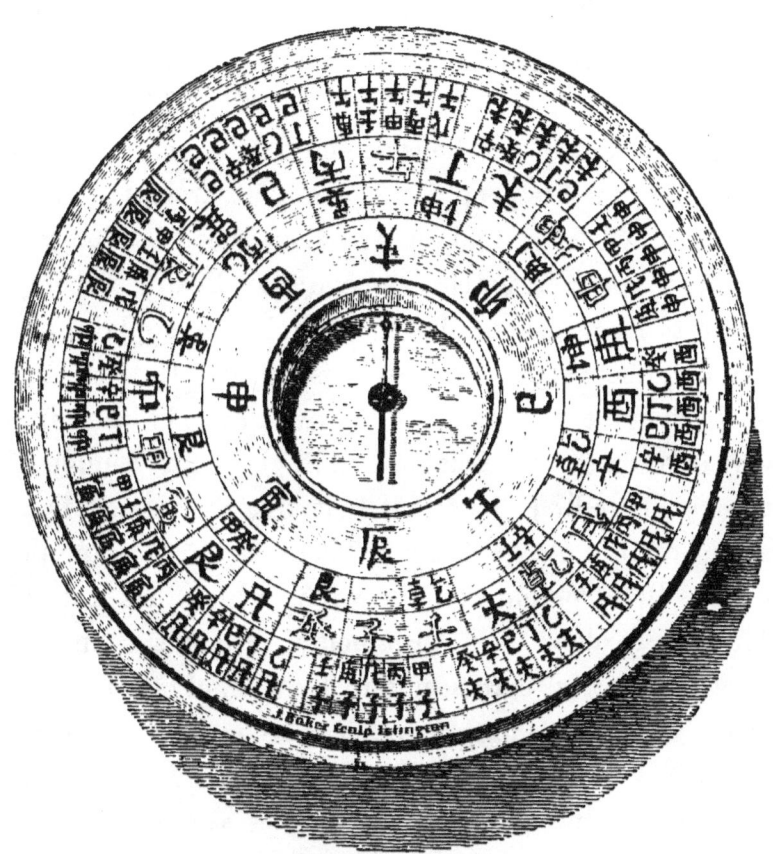

A CHINESE COMPASS.

"Are the houses in Canton all low like those in Pekin?" asked Grace.

"The greater number of them are only one story high, but those of the mandarins and most important merchants are high and well built. The streets are not so wide as those of Pekin, but they are very long, and have arches over them at intervals. Piazzas run along the front of the houses, and form a very pleasant protection, for the people in the streets, from the heat of the sun, besides making the houses cool. The city is much more irregular in shape than Pekin, probably owing to its position. Pekin is built on a plain, but the neighbourhood of Canton is hilly. In fact, the prospect to be seen from some parts of it is beautiful. One of its most remarkable buildings is the Temple of the Five Hundred Gods; but that, like the pagoda, is in a miserable state of decay. There is another temple called the Temple of Longevity, which has capital kitchen gardens and ornamental grounds. In one part of the city there seems to be a kind of park with deer in it, and one traveller who visited the place speaks of having counted thirty head. But he says he expects few strangers were even aware of the existence of the place, for Canton is a most intricate town to find your way about, and that even the inhabitants, when they go far from their own houses, often carry a fan with a plan of the city upon it, and that the wise

CHINESE TEMPLE.

mandarins not unfrequently have a compass in their sedan chairs."

"But have the Chinese compasses?" asked Grace. "It seems to me that they have everything that we have."

"They discovered the compass long before it was known in Europe, but it was not of the same use to them that it has been to European nations. It never gave them any boldness in navigation. Yet the Chinese compasses are singularly well made, being most sensitive to the least movement. The name which the Chinese give to it is ting-nan-ching, which means the needle pointing to the south. We, you know, consider it to point to the north, but while we look at one end, the attention of the Chinese seems to have been caught by the other, for both statements are, of course, equally true."

CHAPTER VIII.

UNDAUNTED BY DIFFICULTIES.

"YOU did not tell us anything about what the missionaries are doing at Pekin, Nankin, and Canton when you were talking about them last time, mamma," said Mabel. "Won't you do so now?"

"There is not very much to tell, my dear, I am afraid; or, at any rate, not much that would interest you. The Church Missionary Society has a station at Pekin, and I believe there is a missionary hospital at Canton; but I cannot find much about either that you would, I think, care to hear. There is more that is interesting to tell, in the way of missionary matter, about some of the other cities of China. In Shanghai, for instance, the Church Missionary Society has had missionaries working for a good many years. For a time they were withdrawn; but in 1870 they went back again. But, you know, the Chinese are a very discouraging people to work among. It is so hard to excite any interest in religious matters. I suppose if you talk to a Chinaman on almost any other topic he will listen to you; but to anything which you may have to say on this most important of all subjects he, too often, turns an utterly indifferent ear. The missionary may, perhaps, work for years, and yet see little fruit from his labours; and it is always hard to go on then, you know."

"I should think missionaries to China ought to be men that don't know what it is to give anything up, and who really like difficulties," said Mabel. "Don't you think so, mamma? Why, it must be the very hardest country in all the world to work in, what with the frightful language, the love of the people for opium, and then this indifference."

"But do you believe there are any people who like difficulties?" inquired Frank. "People may talk about it, and may pretend to like them, but I don't believe anybody ever does."

"Well, perhaps, if there were two ways of reaching one object—the one difficult and the other easy—you would find that every one would choose the easy path," said Mrs. Foster; "yet I am quite sure that there is a great pleasure in overcoming difficulties—a pleasure that lazy and indolent people know nothing of. And some people have a greater appreciation of this pleasure than others, so that nothing daunts them.

"Several of the missionaries who have laboured in China have been men of this kind. Such, for instance, was Dr. Morrison, who translated the Bible into Chinese. Just think of the courage and perseverance that that must have required; and he began it, too, at a time when there seemed little hope of an opening being made for the introduction of Christianity into the country. Then, I read an account the other day of a missionary who died in 1865—only ten years ago—whose dogged perseverance was enough to make every one ashamed of ever saying 'I can't' about anything. His name was Henderson, and he worked at Shanghai as a medical missionary. I will tell you a little about him, because his history will be a good lesson to you all, and will show you boys what a young fellow can do when he has resolutely determined that he will.

"He was a Scotchman, and the child of poor parents, and lost his father when he was only three years old. He had a brother and sister rather older than himself; and his poor widowed mother had a hard struggle to bring her three children up. But she was a good woman, and thankfully accepted the divine invitation, 'Let thy widows trust in Me.' She did trust, and, therefore, was never forsaken. She worked hard, and was able to keep the wolf from the door; and after two years, her father, having lost his wife, asked her to come and live with him. He was a small farmer, and little James was employed in the fields, doing what he could. His mother taught him to read; but he never went to school, and therefore did not learn writing or arithmetic, those accomplishments being considered quite unnecessary by his friends. He had not many books, and therefore, being fond of reading, was forced to read his Bible a great deal. He acquired a great love for its contents, and would often spend hours on Sundays, in some quiet spot, studying the gospels. After three years his grandfather died, and about the same time his mother married again. But her marriage did not improve her lot in a worldly point of view, for her husband was as poor as herself. He was, however, a very excellent man, and was very kind to James, who still continued to live at home until the death of his mother, which occurred when he was about fourteen. He felt this loss most deeply, and at first was almost overwhelmed with grief. But the Bible was his great comfort; and he was enabled to believe that, since his father and mother were dead, the Lord would take him. He now engaged himself to a farmer, to take care of cattle, and after remaining with him for six months, obtained another place of the same kind, in which he remained until he was sixteen. He then became servant to a surgeon, who was exceedingly kind to him, and who, finding that he was anxious to improve himself, procured him instruction in writing and arithmetic, besides lending him good books. However, in this time of outward prosperity, I am sorry to say, he began to wander away from God, and to lose his love for divine things. He got among a set of idle fellows, and soon gave up prayer and the study of his Bible. Conscience told him loudly that he was doing wrong, and warned him to return; but he stopped his ears, and for some time continued to walk, with quicker and quicker steps, in the downward path. God, however, had mercy on him, and before long brought the poor wandering sheep into the safe and happy fold. The first thing that made him stop in his course of folly was the faithful preaching of a minister named Mr. Nicolls, whose church he attended, and whose sermons often made him tremble, and brought him on his knees before God. After a time, too, he obtained a situation in a family where the greatest attention was paid to religious duties. The butler, under whom James was placed, was a sincere and earnest Christian, and his counsel and example were of the greatest use to him. He began resolutely to seek the way of salvation, and soon was able to rejoice in God his Saviour. The question at once began to arise in his mind, 'What can I do for Him who has done so much for me? How can I best serve Him?' His great desire was to become a preacher of the Gospel. But how could he, a poor uneducated lad, obtain the knowledge requisite to qualify him for such a high and holy office? The Church to which he belonged required of those who wished to be ordained a training of eight years. This was enough to frighten any one, and especially one who was already more than twenty, who had never been to school, and who had no money.

"However, James was not daunted. He fully believed the proverb, 'Where there's a will there's a way,' and set manfully to work. At first, the butler was able to help him, for he was a far better scholar than butlers usually are; and when his stock of learning was expended James had recourse to the parish schoolmaster. Thus he went on for some years, studying hard in all his leisure hours, and at the same time saving every penny that he could out of his wages. At the end of five years he made up his mind to leave his situation, that he might devote himself entirely to his books. He took lodgings in a little town, and engaged one of the assistant-masters in a neighbouring school to teach him in the evenings. Here he studied hard for five months, and lived hard, too; for he only allowed himself two meals a day, and seldom spent more than half-a-crown a week on food. At the end of the five months he determined to go to Edinburgh, as he thought he should be able to study better there, and also might there find some situation which would leave him plenty of time to himself, and yet would enable him to gain some money. He was not disappointed, though, of course, such a situation was not to be found in a hurry. For six weeks he wandered about, seeking employment, and at the end of that time God directed him to a situation exactly such as he required. His new mistress was an elderly lady, who needed little service from him beyond keeping her accounts and posting her letters. She paid him excellent wages, so that he was able to save a great deal for future expenses.

"While in Edinburgh he consulted several ministers with regard to his future course, telling them that he wanted to enter the ministry. But, strange to say, they discouraged him, thinking, I suppose, that it would be impossible for him to get through the eight years at the University with apparently no money. Their advice seems to have produced a certain effect upon him. At any rate, at this time he began to think of changing his plan and becoming a doctor instead of a clergyman. He had noticed what great opportunities doctors have for doing good to the souls as well as the bodies of their patients, and the course of study required for that profession is not so long as that for the ministry. In 1855 he entered the Surgeons' Hall, Edinburgh, as a student, but it was not until the close of 1856 that he made up his mind to become a medical missionary. Up to that time his intention had been to do as much good as he could while practising as a doctor at home. But his interest was so much excited at a meeting of the Medical Missionary Society, which took place on the 15th of December in that year, that within twenty-four hours his mind was made up, and he offered himself to the Society. He was of course accepted, and during the last part of his college career the Society paid his educational expenses. He was determined, however, to do the thing thoroughly, and to obtain a doctor's degree, which the Society did not consider necessary for its agents, and was not therefore willing to pay for. However, after all the struggles that James Henderson had gone through, it must have seemed a mere trifle to have to obtain the money requisite for the necessary fees by private pupils, and in 1859 he took his M.D. degree at the University of St. Andrews. There was not at once any opening for him in the missionary field, for at that time the Medical Missionary Society did not itself send men, but only trained and prepared them for other Societies. He therefore, while waiting for a post, began to practise as a country doctor in his native county. Here he met with the most rapid success, and it was evident that if he remained in Great Britain he would soon be a distinguished man. But his heart was set upon working for the Lord in the missionary field, and he did not rest until he had found a post. He offered himself to the London Missionary Society, was accepted, and appointed to go to China. Somewhere about this time a practice worth £700 a year was offered him in the county of Durham; but he had put his hand to the plough and would not look back. He refused the tempting offer, and on the 22nd of October, 1859, sailed for China. The beginning of his voyage was far from being prosperous. After tossing about for fourteen days in the Channel, the ship at length landed its passengers at Portsmouth, and it did not set sail again until the 9th of November. During that period many ships were wrecked; one of which, the *Royal Charter*, some of you may have heard of. It was lost while Henderson's ship, the *Heroes of Alma*, was lying at anchor in the Downs. At length, the 23rd of March, he and several other missionaries who had sailed with him landed at Shanghai. Henderson at once undertook the management of the Chinese hospital, which had then been established for about fourteen years, and was silently exercising a most beneficial influence upon the apathetic people, offering, as it did, an opportunity for the daily preaching of the Gospel to those who flocked to it for the healing of their bodies, and at the same time prepossessing them in favour of the teaching of the white foreigners. Under Dr. Henderson's management the hospital became more popular than ever, and incredible numbers came to it for advice. All who attended heard the news of a Saviour's love, and some, we must hope, received it by a true and living faith. But Dr. Henderson was content to leave the work with God, assured that his word would not return unto Him void. 'In the quiet performance of our daily duties,' he once wrote, ' we are not responsible for our measure of success. Present duty only is ours, events belong to God.' Some one once asked him whether the Chinese were grateful. 'As a rule they are not,' he replied; 'but this is nothing to the purpose, I never came to China to gain the people's gratitude, but to do them good.' Still now and then a letter of thanks would come from some one whom he had cured, or occasionally a present. One man presented six beds to the institution, and sent a very fat goat and four pigeons to Dr. Henderson himself. He also sent a tablet, which he requested might be put up in the hospital to commemorate the year and the month in which the cure was effected. This is a translation of what was on the tablet:—

"'Merit more lofty than Loo or Peen.

"'In the third year of Tung-che (1864), first of the cycle, mid spring month, being afflicted with wind in the liver, which extended to my mouth and eye, and turned them awry, thanks to Hwang-cham-foo, he introduced me to Dr. James Henderson, under whose treatment I was perfectly cured.

"'Dr. Henderson lives for the benefit of humanity, steadily refusing all acknowledgment. Hence I have indited this sentence to be exhibited in this establishment, that so my feeling of gratitude may never be obliterated. Respectfully inscribed by Koo-yne-che, of the city of Paow-shan.'"

"Did many opium smokers come to him?" asked Mabel.

"At first they came in large numbers, but when they found that he would do nothing for them unless they consented to give up their pipes, the numbers became much fewer."

"Do you know, Mrs. Foster," said Frank Mason, "there is a boy at our school who says it is all humbug about the Chinese smoking opium so much? He says his father lived for several weeks at some place in China, and never met with any one who smoked it."

"I can quite understand that," replied Mrs. Foster. "A good many people go to India, and never see any tigers, and yet it would be absurd to say that there are none. They don't see them because they don't look for them. And then the Chinese are almost always ashamed of the habit, and are very long before they will confess to it. It is not often that you will find a man in England acknowledge that he is a drunkard; and just in the same way, the opium-smokers try to conceal their vice. You require to live among the people for a long time, and to know them very thoroughly, before you find out the true state of the case.

"But I must go on, and tell you a little more about Dr. Henderson. Of course, his work at the hospital must have pretty well filled up his time, for the numbers that came for advice steadily increased. Still he found time for other things. In the winter of 1863-4 he gave a course of lectures to the English soldiers, chiefly on historical subjects. He also assembled around him, on Sunday evenings, a number of young English merchants, for the study of the Scriptures and prayer. Some of these young fellows he seems to have been warmly attached to; and, no doubt, his friendship and counsel was of the greatest benefit to them."

"But is he dead, mamma?" said Grace. "You keep on saying 'was' and 'did' about everything, as if the work was all over and done."

"And so, as far as Dr. Henderson was concerned, it is, my dear. His work in China was very short. He arrived in Shanghai in 1860, and died in 1865."

"Did he, mamma—so soon as that? How strange it seems, doesn't it? When he had had such a hard struggle to become a doctor, and when he was doing so much good! Doesn't it seem strange that God did not let him live a little longer?"

"Perhaps it does, Grace," replied Mrs. Foster; "but then, you know, there are so many things that we do not understand. No doubt, the poor sick people in Shanghai, and all his friends there, felt that they could not possibly do without Dr. Henderson; but

God took him away, and they had to. And other people were raised up to do his work; and people were taught not to trust in an arm of flesh, but only in the living God.

"Dr. Henderson seems to have thought it probable that his life would be a short one. 'I shall not be surprised,' he said, in one of his letters, 'if I do not live to be thirty-six.' And he did not. In the spring of 1865 he became very much overdone with his work, and made up his mind to go for change to Japan. But when the time drew near for his departure, a great reluctance came over him, and he seemed to have a presentiment that he should never return. Indeed, on bidding farewell to his Chinese assistant, he said, 'Good-bye, Chu-foo; I shall never come back again.' The low fever from which he suffered produced extreme weakness, and the sea breezes did not do the good which the doctors had fondly hoped they might. After he landed in Japan he became gradually worse. All the kindness of doctors and friends, and the tender nursing of his wife, were of no avail. The good fight was fought, the crown was ready, and on the 30th of July the soldier was called to enter into his rest.

"He was buried in Nangasaki, and almost every foreigner in the place attended his funeral. The grief felt in Shanghai, when the news of his death arrived, you can imagine. Not only did his personal friends sorrow for their own loss, but every one felt that the poor Chinese had lost their best friend."

"I should think so," said Grace; "and don't you think, mamma, that very often a doctor must do more good among the heathen than a clergyman, especially when the people are like the Chinese, and don't care to be talked to about their souls? I suppose people will often listen when they are sick, who would not care at all for anything that you might say to them when they are well. And then, when people see that a doctor can do their bodies good, and that he does not ask for any money, they must see quite well that he wants to do them good, and that he knows more than they do. It seems, too, so like the way in which the Lord Jesus gathered the people around Him. They came to Him to have their sick people healed, and then He preached to them and taught them."

"That is what the people who established the Medical Missionary Society thought; and I believe many of their missions have proved very successful. As you say, people's hearts are often softer when they are ill and suffering. The Chinese ideas about diseases and medicine are very absurd; and as they consider the study of anatomy wrong, they cannot, of course, be good surgeons. A missionary gives an account of a poor man whom he found suffering from dropsy. He was very ill, and required the most skilful treatment; but the native doctors who attended him considered the cause of his illness to be a little drop of coagulated blood, which was circulating, and must be expelled before the poor man could hope to be any better. And what do you imagine was one of the remedies prescribed?"

"Something very filthy, I dare say," said Mabel. "What was it, mamma?"

"A course of toads, my dear. I do not know whether they are as nice as the French people consider frogs; but I should think they can hardly be good for a man suffering from a liver complaint. His friends could not be brought to let him be treated by an English doctor, and he died in a very short time."

"And no wonder either," said Tom. "But what sort of a place is Shanghai?"

"I do not know that there is anything very distinctive about it. It is surrounded by a wall, like the other towns which I have described to you, and has six gates. It is on the sea coast, and, in a commercial point of view, is a place of the greatest importance. The country all round is very well cultivated, cotton being the principal thing that is grown. There are no particular buildings that you would care to hear about. There are, of course, a good many temples, but none that are very remarkable. But in one part of the city there is a triumphal arch to the honour of a man called Sen, who was a person of great importance in the seventeenth century, and, though a Christian, rose to the highest honours of the State. His descendants are some of them Christians and some of them Pagans. The Pagans have erected an altar to his memory, and worship his image. His tomb, outside the city, is attended to with the greatest care, and seven regularly planted trees grow on it; no little saplings either, but trees of gigantic size."

"Have not the Chinese some very strange customs about their burials?" inquired Grace. "Don't they leave the coffins uncovered?"

"I believe they do, until the time of mourning is over; then a few shovelfuls of earth are put upon it, and the next year a few more, and so on, until a mound arises, and rank grass and Chinese lilies spring up. Some writers speak of hills only being set apart for this purpose; and here is the picture of a burial-place near the Yellow River, which certainly is on the

BURIAL PLACE, NEAR THE YELLOW RIVER.

side of a hill, and where there are regularly built tombs; but the Marquis de Beauvoir, and other modern travellers, speak of having seen acres and acres of land in the neighbourhood of Shanghai dotted over with coffins. Yet the tract of land in which they are to be seen is not wholly given up to them. There are villages among them, and the ground around is cultivated, and you may not unfrequently see a coffin lying in the midst of a field of cabbages. The coffins, you know, are not plain deal or oaken boxes, like those used in England, but are richly carved, and they are fastened down by a plaster called 'chunam,' which is thought to keep the air effectually out. Whether it does or not, I cannot say; but some travellers describe the atmosphere of the country I have been talking about as very disagreeable and death-like. The Chinese have the greatest objection to removing a coffin, and this has been a serious obstacle in the way of the construction of railways and telegraphs. A telegraph, indeed, was set up for some miles by an important merchant, in order to give notice of the arrival of mails and ships; but in a few days it was cut in several places, just because it cast its shadow on some coffins."

"What an absurd idea!" said Tom. "Only fancy doing without such useful things as railways and telegraphs for such a reason as that! But Shanghai is just at the mouth of the Yang-tze-kiang, isn't it? So, perhaps, the people do not feel the need of railways so much as they would if they had not such a splendid river. It is the longest in the Old World, isn't it?"

"Yes, I believe it is. But you are mistaken in imagining that Shanghai is directly on it. It stands on the bank of a little river called the Woosung, and is about twelve miles from the Yang-tze-kiang."

"Is it really, mamma? Why, on the map, it looks as if it was quite close."

"But you must remember what a large country China is, and that unless you have a very large map indeed, a distance of twelve miles would be scarcely perceptible. The Chinese empire, you know, extends over more than a fourth part of Asia, and is bigger than the whole of Europe."

"Oh, yes, I know," said Tom; "and is not its population said to be something enormous—about one-third of all the people in the world, or something like it?"

"Well, that is what has long been popularly supposed," replied Mrs. Foster. "But now that the country is more open to foreigners, and people have been able to explore it better, it seems doubtful whether there are anything like so many people in it as was thought. Some parts, I believe, are densely populated; and then, again, hundreds of miles are almost uninhabited, so that some modern travellers say the population has been enormously exaggerated. But it is very difficult to find out anything certain about it."

"I sometimes begin to wonder whether one ought to believe anything," said Mabel, "at least about geography, and things of that sort. I am sure I have often taken elaborate pains to get something into my head, and then after a little time have been pretty sure to hear that it was all a mistake. And then, too, different books say such different things. Yesterday I was learning my geography lesson, and was very much surprised to find that the book said that the Mississippi was the longest river in the world. I knew that I had learnt some other name, so I looked in the geography book that I used some time ago, and sure enough there I found it said that the Amazon was the largest river in the world. So, if it is a mistake about China having such an enormous number of people in it, perhaps, by-and-by, people will find out that the Yang-tze-kiang is not a big river at all, only a little mill-stream."

"Hardly that, I think," replied Mrs. Foster, smiling. "I cannot say; perhaps it may have to descend from its honourable position as the longest river in the Old World; for, as you say, geographers do differ in their decisions, but all the wise men in the world could not prove the Yang-tze-kiang to be anything but a very long river. It and the Hoang-ho rise very near to one another, and then their streams diverge so much from that one point, they are more than a thousand miles apart. But they approach each other again towards their mouths, and are only about a hundred miles apart when they empty themselves into the sea. At one part of the river, I should think probably near the mouth, it is no less than three miles wide, and has within it an island called Chin-san, or the Golden Island. Here is a picture of it. It belongs to the Emperor, and has some beautiful gardens on it. There is also a large monastery for priests, who are almost the sole inhabitants of the island. There is a ship, you see, in the picture, and it is a very good representation of a Chinese ship-of-war."

"Well, I should think they must be rather funny things, then," said Frank. "It does not look half so nice as our ships. What are the Chinese ships like? They are called junks, are they not?"

"Yes," replied Mrs. Foster. "I do not know that I can give you a very good account of them, for I do not

THE GOLDEN ISLAND.

know much about nautical matters, and very likely I shall make mistakes that will amuse you boys. But I will do my best. In the account of the embassy that took place at the end of the last century, and which, I dare say, you will remember I mentioned to you some time ago, the writer describes the junks which came to receive the presents intended for the Emperor. He says that the contrast between them and the towering masts and complicated tackling of the English men-of-war was very singular. The junks are low, simple, and clumsy, but strong and roomy. The holds are divided into compartments by partitions of wood, and all the seams are caulked with a cement of lime which won't let the water in, and won't burn."

"But what is the use of doing that?" inquired Frank. "I don't see what is the good of it, and it must take up so much room."

"Of course it does do that, and for that reason, I suppose, European merchantmen would never adopt such a plan; but it has its advantages. One merchant's goods may suffer seriously from a leak in one compartment, and all other goods be conveyed quite safely. Then, too, a ship may strike upon a rock, and yet not sink, for the water which gets in at the hole is confined to the division where the damage happened to be.

"A junk, I believe, generally has two masts, which are much thicker in proportion to their length than those in our ships. It is much the same shape at both ends, neither of them being sharp and pointed. The rudder is placed at one end, and the compass is enclosed in a bowl, and stands much in the same position as it does in European ships. A light is often kept near it, and a quantity of sand is placed in the bowl, in which a number of perfumed matches are stuck when an offering is to be made to the god of the sea. There is always an altar, too, to this god on board a junk, and near it are the berths of the captain and crew, all as small as they can be made. Each berth has a mat on it by way of a bed, and a very hard cushion for the head. Sometimes the crew of a junk will contain as many as forty or fifty men; and in the merchant ships, I believe, they are not paid any fixed wages, but each man receives a portion of the profits arising from the voyage performed.

"But really, my dear children, we must not talk any more, for it is high time that the work was put away."

CHAPTER IX.

HANG-CHOW.

IF you remember, children, we were talking, the last time we met, about the Chinese ships, and since that time I have met with a picture, which I thought at once you would like to see. Here it is. You see there is only one man to manage the boat; but apparently he has discovered how to do a good many things at one and the same time. With one hand, you see, he steers, and with the other manages the sail, while he pulls a large oar with his foot, and smokes all the time most coolly, as if he did not at all feel that he had too much to do. On the river Chen-lang-Chiang, near Hang-choo-foo, I believe quite large boats are managed in this manner."

"But I do not in the least see how any one can possibly row with his foot," said Tom. "He might push the oar one way; but how could he possibly bring it back again?"

"I don't understand it either," replied Mrs. Foster;

" but neither can I comprehend how people paint with their feet, and yet I know it is done. There is nothing like practice; and there are few things which people cannot do when they try.

" But I do not mean to make boats the subject of my talk to you this afternoon, but want to tell you a little about Ningpo."

" That is on the coast of China, too, isn't it, mamma?" said Mabel. "You do not tell us anything about the places that lie inland."

" That is a mistake, my dear; for Pekin is an inland city. But it is not easy to gain much information about the interior of the country; for you must not forget that it is only very recently that there has been anything like free access to China. The reason why I am going to tell you anything about Ningpo is because it is one of the treaty ports, and missionaries have been working there for a considerable time. In a commercial point of view, it is not apparently a place of much importance; for neither much silk nor much tea is shipped from it. But a good many carpets and mats are made there, and a great many of the women are employed in weaving cloth. As a learned city, however, it ranks as quite one of the highest in the country, no less than one-fifth of the population being estimated as belonging to the literary class. The city, like those that I have before described, is surrounded by a wall, and has six gates. The streets are wide and clean, and there are a great many temples in it; but it is quite plain that the place is not by any means so important or imposing as it used to be, there are so many empty and decaying houses. But the people are kind, peaceable, and friendly, and the climate, though extremely cold in the winter and hot in the summer, is tolerably healthy to Europeans."

"You have never told us anything about the climate of China at all yet, mamma," said Grace. "Is it as hot as India?"

"I think if you were to consider for a few minutes, my dear, you would see that the climate of such a large country must vary very much. At Hong-kong, for instance, the thermometer is seldom below 50°, while at Pekin the cold in winter is very intense, and people find it hard to keep themselves warm. A missionary's wife once showed me a dress which she said she found most comfortable there. It was entirely made of fur, and lined with silk. On the very cold days, she said, she wore it with the fur turned inside; and when the weather was not quite so severe, she turned it the other side outwards. The cold at Ningpo is very nearly as great, the thermometer sometimes going down to 18°. But, both at Ningpo and Pekin, the heat in summer is also very great. In some other places, however, it is much more temperate; and, I suppose, in China you can find, in fact, almost any climate you like. Then, too, the vegetation is extremely various. In one part it is all tropical; and in another you may see dog-roses and wild honeysuckle. In spring, I believe, the hills near Ningpo are bright with many-coloured azaleas."

"How beautiful they must look, must not they, mamma?" said Mabel. "Is the country round Ningpo fine?"

"From what I can gather, I should think it is. The White Mountain is in its immediate vicinity, and travellers speak of the view to be obtained from its summit as very striking."

"Is not the island of Chusan somewhere near Ningpo?"

"Yes; and you can see it from the top of the White Mountain. It is a beautiful island, and some people think it is a pity that we have not got possession of it instead of Hong-kong. Its position is a much more commanding one; and for a few months we did hold it, but exchanged it for Hong-kong. One of its inhabitants expressed the patriotic wish to an English traveller who

A MANDARIN'S GARDEN AT CHUSAN.

visited it a few years ago, that his countrymen would come and take it again. So I suppose our rule, while we held it, was not very tyrannical—less so, perhaps, than the paternal despotism of their own Emperor. A curious instance of the arbitrary manner in which people are made to do what they are told occurred some years ago in this same island. It was at the time of that embassy which I have mentioned to you several times. The ambassador and his train landed at Chusan, and after being received with the greatest honour and respect by the governor, inquired for some pilots, to pilot them to Tien-sing. A long speech was made in reply, with an immense display of eloquence, the drift of which was that no pilots were to be had at Chusan, it being only a subsidiary part to Ningpo; but that if the ambassador would follow the Chinese method, and keep along the coast, no pilots would be necessary. The ambassador did not consider this advisable, and replied simply that he would at once repair to Ningpo, and procure pilots there. But to this proposition the governor offered the strongest resistance, saying that it would bring upon him the heaviest displeasure of the Emperor, who would at once conclude that the reception at Chusan had been unsatisfactory, and would probably deprive him of his office and dignity;

and the poor man pointed, in the most pathetic manner, to the red button on his cap, which denoted that he belonged to the second of the nine classes of magistrates. What was to be done? The ambassador did not feel disposed to risk the safety of the ships by going without pilots, and yet was unwilling to bring so much trouble upon the unfortunate mandarin. But the mandarin himself solved the difficulty. He sent people scouring about the island, to bring before him all the men who had ever made the voyage to Tien-sing. They were at once examined as to their skill in navigation; and at last two men were found who were pronounced quite capable of conducting the squadron. But these poor unfortunate fellows were most unwilling to go, and prostrated themselves before the governor, imploring him to excuse them. Their families and their businesses, they said, required their presence at home. Could they not be let off? But the governor was inexorable. The will of the Emperor, he said, must be done; and the poor men had to go."

"What a shame!" exclaimed Tom. "I hope they were well paid."

"I am sure I cannot tell you; but I should think probably they were. The ambassador would very much have preferred procuring pilots from Ningpo; but, you see, he could not help himself. However, we have got quite away from Ningpo, and I wanted to tell you a little about the missionary work there. It was in that city, you remember, that Miss Aldersey for so many years carried on her girls' school. But she did not confine herself to work among the girls, but did all she could in any way that offered itself to promote the knowledge of salvation. Among other things she rented a small house in a village about four miles and a half from Ningpo, called Ly-kyi-du, near to the large town of Tsong-gyiao, and in this house a native catechist used every week to preach the Gospel, going out from Ningpo for the purpose. For a year or two the work went on, but no fruit appeared, and it was determined to remove the preaching to the town itself. Very soon after this change had been made, an inquirer appeared. His name was Dzao-tch-sing, but he was commonly called Bong-s-vu, which means 'a maker of bamboo tilt,' something for covering boats. I do not suppose, however much I may try, that I shall pronounce either of his names properly, but, as the second one is the shorter of the two, I shall call him Bong-s-vu. Well, Bong-s-vu said that, one day, as he was passing through the town, he saw a large crowd, and stopped to see what was going on. It was the catechist preaching, and he had taken the Ten Commandments for his text. Bong-s-vu's heart was touched, and his interest excited, and he wanted to know more. The catechist explained to him 'the way of life more fully,' he received the glad tidings with simple faith, and was baptized in January, 1860. The next year he spent quietly working at his trade, but at the same time diligently studying his Bible. 1861 was a year of great disturbances, there being a rebellion going on in China at that time. The town of Ningpo was taken by the rebels, who swept over the whole province. Bong-s-vu was obliged to leave his home, and took his wife and family to a part of the country called the Eastern Lakes District. It was here that his wife's relations lived, and while he stayed among them Bong-s-vu was diligent in trying to win them to the Saviour; and his labours were abundantly blessed, for when the missionaries were able to visit the district, which they did in 1862, they found the old mother, an uncle of the wife's, and her three brothers, all earnestly desiring baptism—in fact, the foundation of a church laid. With the help of the Christians in Ningpo, the little band of converts now rented a room, and a catechist was sent out each Sunday either from

Ningpo or Tsong-gyiao to conduct a service. But soon it was found desirable to have a resident agent, and after some months trial Bong-s-vu was appointed catechist. Here he laboured most diligently until within a few years of his death, and then it was deemed expedient to remove him to En-ling, a large town on the further shores of the lake."

"And did he do a great deal there, mamma?" said Grace. "I should think he must have been sorry to go away from his own friends and relations."

"Probably he was, but doubtless he felt glad to go to any place where there seemed to be work to be done for his Saviour. At any rate, while at En-ling, it may be truly said of him, that 'he ceased not to teach and preach Jesus Christ.' Yet the apparent fruit of his labours was small, only five men being baptized during Bong-s-vu's lifetime. I say apparent, for I don't think the result of any work can be judged of at the time that it is going on, or even immediately afterwards. Sometimes the seed is in the ground many days before it springs up.

Bong-s-vu was not an educated man, and did not know how to read at the time of his conversion to Christianity, but with such ardour did he apply himself to study, that long before his death he could read the New Testament both in the Chinese character and in the Romanized colloquial."

"What do you mean by that, mamma?" said Mabel. "What is the Romanized colloquial?"

"You remember, I told you that though there is only one written language in China, there are a great many spoken languages. Now some of these languages the missionaries have lately reduced to writing by means of the same alphabet that we use."

"I suppose they did it because they thought they would be easier to learn than the regular, proper language, did not they, mamma?"

"No doubt that was the reason," replied Mrs. Foster; "but as I just said, Bong-s-vu learnt both the colloquial of the district and also the regular written language. He was, too, a most diligent student of the Bible, and the missionary under whose guidance and control he was placed says he shall 'never forget the thoughtful papers brought up by him month after month, when the catechists assembled at his house for Bible lectures on the Thirty-nine Articles.' This earnestness in study of course helped to make him a thorough teacher, and the candidates whom he from time to time presented for baptism were always remarkably well prepared."

"Bong-s-vu died in the hospital at Ningpo. He had for some time been suffering from a very painful disease, and the missionary pressed him to come to Ningpo, in order that he might see an English doctor. But he did not live many days after his arrival. His little boy waited upon him during the last few days of his life, and the child's account of his death was very touching. He said that on the last night he sat up until the early morning. His father then begged him to go to bed, and being no doubt very sleepy and tired, he complied. But he awoke about daybreak and got up, in order to give his father some medicine. His father seemed to be asleep, but when the little fellow called there was no answer. He touched his hand and found it cold. Bong-s-vu needed no more medicine, he had laid his poor suffering body down, and had entered into his eternal rest. The grief of the little boy, as you can imagine, was very great, and he cried most bitterly as he told his story to the missionary."

"I am sure I don't wonder," said Mabel. "What a shock it must have given him! I think it must be so dreadful to wake up and find the person you have been taking care of dead. Do you know what has become of the little boy, mamma? Has he grown up to be a good man?"

"I should think he has scarcely grown up at all yet," said Mrs. Foster, " for it was only in 1871 that Bong-s-vu died. But I do not really know anything about him."

"Is not it very difficult indeed to be sure whether a Chinese has become a Christian or not?" inquired Frank. "I heard some one say yesterday, that he doubted whether any Chinese had ever really become a Christian; though a good many had of course persuaded the missionaries that they had."

"That was, I should think, the same gentleman who said it was all a mistake about the opium," said Mrs. Foster. "There undoubtedly have been many, though I suppose it is more necessary to be cautious in speaking certainly of Chinese than of almost any people. There is such a want of truth in the national character, and they are so scrupulously polite, that those who do not know them well are apt to be deceived."

"You mean that the Chinese will profess to be Christians just to please people?"

"I am afraid they will, sometimes. A missionary once, after talking for a long time to a man who had most patiently listened to all that was said, thinking he would see how much effect his words had produced, said, 'Now, do you believe in the Lord Jesus Christ?' 'Most certainly I do,' was the prompt, polite reply.

"'But why do you believe?' pursued the missionary; 'are you really convinced? Do you feel that what I have been saying is true?' 'I believe it because you say so,' was the polite and hopeless answer."

"And, of course, he did not really believe at all?" said Mabel. "What very provoking sort of people they must be to have to do with! I know, if I was a missionary, I would much rather have the people actively oppose me than assent to what I might say in that cool, indifferent sort of way. But I suppose that would be too much trouble. They are lazy people, are not they?"

"No, I do not think they are at all that," replied Mrs. Foster. "On the contrary, I believe they are remarkably industrious, and I have heard that they make excellent servants. They feel little interest in the matter of religion, and therefore do not care to oppose. But it is quite a mistake to think that they shrink from trouble. As the traveller goes through the crowded streets of the great towns, one thing which specially strikes him is the great activity of the people, and the way in which everything is turned to account. And it is just the same in the country districts. Everybody seems to work as diligently as possible; even the buffaloes, who are sometimes used in the farm work, are not suffered a moment's idleness. I do not mean, though, that the poor animals are treated cruelly, for I don't think that they are."

"They grow a great deal of rice in China, don't they, Mrs. Foster?" inquired Frank.

"Yes; as in India, I suppose it is the principal article of food with a large part of the population. It is a grain, you know, which requires a great quantity of moisture, and the Chinese have invented some very ingenious machines for watering the land. One of them, called the scoop wheel, which is very common in the southern provinces, will raise nearly 70,000 gallons of water in twenty-four hours. It is made entirely of bamboo, and is put together without a nail. Here is the picture of a kind of chain pump, which is used for draining land or for raising water to a small height out of rivers or canals. You see it is worked with the feet, just like the treadmill. Then they have another, which is called 'the sitting wheel,' because the labourer works it while sitting down. A third kind is set in motion with the hand, and is therefore called the hand wheel; and a fourth, and more complicated one, is worked by a buffalo."

WATER-WHEEL.

"But can they really make a buffalo work a wheel like that?" said Tom. "I should have thought it was too big and stupid."

"Of course the buffalo does not work it in the same way as men do. He could not exactly manage a treadmill, I fancy. He turns round a horizontal wheel, which, by means of cogs, turns, in its turn, the roller which raises the water. It is difficult to make it clear to you, but I dare say some of you boys who are fond of machinery will understand what I mean; and if the girls don't, they must be content to do without.

"However, I am going to tell you a little now about a town called Hang-chow. It is not very far from Ningpo, and is the capital of the province in which it stands, Ningpo being the principal port. The Church Missionary Society began a mission there in 1859, but had to give it up almost immediately. In 1865 they tried again, and the work has been going on ever since. Between 1859 and 1865, the city was taken and sacked by the rebels, who were guilty of the most horrible barbarities, sparing no one who came in their way. It is described, before the capture, as having been a fine and beautifully situated city, placed in the midst of very picturesque scenery, and full of fine buildings. But after its sacking by the rebels, the missionary mourns over the sad spectacle which it presented. Four-fifths of the city are said to have been destroyed, and about the same proportion of the inhabitants perished. It was partly the wretched condition of the place which decided the missionaries to begin a mission there at the time when they did. Two of the native catechists pressed it very much, as they looked upon the time of distress as a favourable one for offering to their apathetic countrymen the comfort of the gospel. The missionary staff at that time was weak, and scarcely sufficient for the work already undertaken, and yet it seemed hardly right to say 'No,' when there was this call. At length it was decided that one of the missionaries, Mr. Moule, accompanied by these two catechists, should, at any rate, make an exploratory expedition. The day before they set out a very curious thing occurred. A Chinese gentleman, a heathen, called upon Mr. Moule, and after asking whether it was really true that he was going to Hangchow, said that a brother of his had both houses and land there, and would most willingly receive Mr. Moule as tenant if he wished for a house in Hangchow, adding, that he supposed the missionaries would certainly seize the opportunity afforded by the pacification at once to commence mission work in Hangchow. Now, Mr. Moule had felt that whether or not

Hang-chow should be occupied, must be dependent upon whether accommodation of any kind could be procured, and this unexpected offer looked like the very guidance he was seeking. He started off on his expedition, carrying with him a letter of introduction to the person mentioned. He was received most civilly, and a large unoccupied house at once placed at his disposal, either to rent or, if he only intended to make a short stay in the place, as a loan. Mr. Moule accepted the latter offer, thinking that it would be better, I suppose, to look about him a little before he finally decided to establish a regular mission in the place. He stayed there about nine days, going about with catechists, talking to the people, and distributing books, and at the end of that time he determined to take the house which had been offered him, and to leave the catechists behind him. The house was not situated in the best position for a preaching place, and therefore he also took a small shop with a room above it in a busy street; and here the work was begun. The two catechists, Dzang and Ts'e, worked diligently, and Mr. Moule frequently received encouraging letters from them. From time to time he paid them visits, and about a year after the work had been first entered upon, decided to remove thither with his whole family. This was a step which required some courage and faith, for there was no European doctor in the place, or anywhere within reach. However, he felt it was the right thing to do, and he says that the presence of his children in the place helped him in his work. The people felt that he was treating them with trust and confidence, and therefore were the more disposed to listen to what he had to say. There seem to have been a great many inquirers from the very beginning of the work, and Mr. Moule speaks of their showing more earnestness than those in Ningpo. Some of those who wished to know fully about Christianity were highly educated men, and one, named Tai, astonished Mr. Moule very much by displaying a thorough knowledge of Romanism. He had studied the doctrines of that Church for five years with the intention of being baptized; but having become acquainted with some of the London missionaries, during a visit to Shanghai, he had found out that the Romish teaching was wrong, and now was anxious to learn from the Protestant missionaries. The first baptism took place about two months after Mr. Moule's removal to Hang-chow, and by that time there were a good many more desiring baptism."

"And would not the missionaries let them be baptized?" inquired little Lucy. "I should have thought they would only be too glad."

"And so they would if they had been quite sure that the people knew what they were doing, and were thoroughly sincere. But they were very anxious to prevent, as much as possible, any professing themselves Christians whose hearts were not really turned to God."

"But I do not see, mamma, how missionaries, or any one else, can ever tell whether that is the case or not," said Grace. "They cannot see into people's hearts."

"Of course they cannot, my dear," replied Mrs. Foster, "but they can watch their lives. 'By their fruits ye shall know them,' our Lord said, and that is what the missionaries look at. When a man comes to them and asks to be baptized, they not only question him to see whether he knows with his head what the religion is that he wishes to profess, but they watch his conduct in order to see whether the fruits of the Spirit are at all beginning to show themselves. Some people indeed, I believe, do think that our Church missionaries are too cautious in admitting people to baptism, but, for my part, I think it is better to be too cautious than too eager. Of course every zealous missionary would be delighted to be able to feel that souls had been won to the Saviour by his efforts, and the temptation to be easily satisfied about people's sincerity and earnestness must be often very great, and yet how much harm a hollow-hearted or even lukewarm professor must do to an infant church!"

"But, mamma," urged Grace, "when one reads the Acts of the Apostles, it never seems as if people were kept waiting then. Very often people seem to have been baptized directly after first hearing about the Saviour, and I don't see why it should be different now."

"Well, for my part," said Mrs. Foster, "I think there was a good deal to make a course of action right then, which would not be altogether wise now. First, the Apostles by whom the gospel was first preached were inspired men, and had a greater power of discerning spirits than is possessed by men of the present day. Then, too, the gift of the Holy Ghost was frequently accompanied by some outward sign, by which His presence might be known; and lastly, the new religion was one despised by both the Jews and the Greeks, and those who professed it were likely to have to bear persecution for their faith. And then, too, you must not forget the awful fate of two false professors in the very early days of the Christian Church. No doubt the fearful deaths of Ananias and Sapphira would deter any, who were not thoroughly in earnest, from professing themselves Christians. Indeed we read, 'And of the rest durst no man join himself unto them.'

"However, the clock is striking, and we must break up for to-day."

CHAPTER X.

HONGKONG AND THE TAEPINGS.

"HAVE the Chinese any amusements, mamma?" said Tom. "I can scarcely imagine John Chinaman doing anything very lively. Just think, Mabel, of the long-tailed fellow waltzing with his small-footed wife! Do they dance at all, mamma? I do not quite see how the ladies can if they find it so hard to walk."

"No," replied Mrs. Foster, "it is a curious fact that China is one of the few countries where there is nothing at all like dancing. Indeed there is, I believe, no word in the language that properly signifies dancing. What the reason of it is I am sure I cannot tell you, for the custom is almost universal, both among civilized and savage nations.

"Perhaps it is because the ladies can't dance. I should think the gentlemen would not care to dance by themselves," said Frank.

"But, in other countries," said Mrs. Foster,

"there are many dances in which men and women dance alone, so I should think that can scarcely be the reason. In fact, it is only among highly civilized nations that men and women dance together. It is only among them, too, that dancing is looked upon simply in the light of an amusement. Very often, among savages, dancing is a religious act. In fact, I suppose, most heathen nations have their religious dances. However, the Chinese, as I said just now, have nothing of the kind, either as a religious service or an amusement.

"Still, they are not without their entertainments. At a feast given to some English visitors on one occasion at Canton, one of the number speaks of a sing-song, or drama, being acted during the dinner for the amusement of those at table. It was accompanied by some genuine Chinese music, and consisted of long dialogues, songs, feats of strength, tumbling, and other muscular exercises. Apparently, one favourite subject for acting is the career of a certain wicked mandarin named Tsaou-Tsaou, who was a kind of Napoleon, and upset the reigning Emperor, founding a new dynasty in the person of his grandson.

"But however fond the people in general may be of

A CHINESE ACTOR.

watching dramatic performances, no encouragement is offered to any one to become an actor. The class, indeed, are looked down upon and despised, and actors, priests, and servants are not allowed to present themselves at the literary examinations, and therefore are excluded from all hope of rising to a position of wealth and importance."

"Are not the Chinese rather great at making fireworks?" inquired Frank. "I think I have heard so."

"I dare say you have," replied Mrs. Foster. "The natives of both India and China are remarkable for their pyrotechnic skill."

"Oh, mamma, what a long word!" said Grace. "Whatever did you use it for?"

"Just that some of you young people might learn its meaning. Try and remember now that the art of making fireworks is called pyrotechny. The feast of lanterns, which is kept about February, seems to be a great occasion for having grand displays of fireworks, and the sights that are to be seen then would delight you. I will try and describe one gigantic and elaborate firework, that a missionary speaks of having seen at one of these feasts. A long pole, fifty feet high, was erected, hung round with cases of rockets and other combustibles. This pole was lighted from the bottom, and there was a rapid succession of squibs, roman candles, guns, and rockets. Then, as I suppose the fire ascended, a house suddenly dropped from one of the arms of the pole, and all the more insignificant fireworks poured in upon it, and completely riddled it. As the house disappeared, a beautiful bunch of grapes came into existence, which shed a deep blue light on all the surrounding objects. This passed away, and then came a shower of golden rain, in the midst of which an umbrella of fire suddenly flew open. Then followed a human figure, which went round and round with the greatest rapidity, all the time being fired at by crackers. The whole thing was concluded by a slanting shower of gold and silver rain, with rockets going through it straight up into the sky."

"How beautiful it must have looked!" exclaimed Tom; "but I suppose it cost a lot of money."

"No doubt it did, but it seems to be the custom regularly to levy contributions in the towns to pay for the fireworks that are let off at the feast of lanterns; and rich men generally spend a good deal on private displays. In fact, the feast of lanterns, apparently, is the occasion of a general jollification, and no expense seems grudged. Shows of all kinds go on, the usual penalties against gambling are relaxed, and, for the

SCENE FROM A CHINESE PLAY.

time, the apathetic Chinaman gives himself up to merry-making."

"But why is it called the feast of lanterns? It seems such an odd name."

"I suppose it is because the houses are illuminated with lanterns. You all know, no doubt, what the Chinese lanterns are like. Well, on this occasion there is an extraordinary display of them. They are to be seen of every conceivable shape and design. Some are made of glass, some of glue, and some of paper; some are in the shape of birds, some of beasts, some of fishes. In fact, the variety and the ingenuity displayed in their construction is something extraordinary. The great thing at this feast seems to be to procure plenty of light, and in all the principal temples, and in the houses of rich men, huge candles are burnt, some of them two feet in circumference. Enormous bonfires, too, are kept blazing, and it is considered to bring good luck to leap across them. On this day of general rejoicing, even the women are allowed a great deal more liberty than usual. They come out of their houses to see the illuminations, and some of them even mingle in the processions which are made to the different idol temples. The temple to which more women go than any other on this night is the one dedicated to the goddess 'Mother,' and they go there to pray for little boys. They always bring away some relic of the goddess, which they keep as a most precious treasure, and worship for the rest of the year."

"I suppose they never pray for little girls," said Grace, "if they look upon their birth as such a misfortune?"

"Most certainly not," replied Mrs. Foster. "Boys are what the Chinese women want; and if they only pay proper devotion to the relic, they think the goddess is sure to grant their prayers."

"But I should think they must be pretty often disappointed?" said Tom. "I suppose, then, they think there has been something wrong in their worship? But tell us something about the games of the children now, mamma. Have they the same kind of games that we have—cricket, and that sort of thing?"

"Well, I never heard of Chinese playing at cricket; but I am afraid I can tell you but very little about the amusements of the young. I believe they are fond of kites; but the men fly them, I fancy, as much as the children. The shuttlecock, too, is a favourite toy, at least with the natives of Cochin China, and the customs of the two countries are very much the

NATIVES OF COCHIN CHINA PLAYING AT SHUTTLECOCK.

same, so that I think it is very probably used in China too."

"Cochin China is somewhere pretty close to China, isn't it?" said Frank. "It is one of that little knot of countries to the east of India that are such a bother to remember. There are Siam, and Burmah, and Tonquin, and Cambodia. I never can keep them straight in my head. But Tonquin is just south of China, isn't it? and Cochin China is just south of that."

"Quite right, Frank. Well, the people of Cochin China very much resemble the Chinese. They use chop-sticks, and drink rice wine, and eat a great deal of rice. But they are gayer and more talkative, and the poor ladies are not condemned to small feet. But I ought not to forget to tell you that they do not play with the shuttlecocks as people play in England. They do not use battledores, but their feet."

"Do you mean that they kick the shuttlecocks up?"

"Yes. I think it must look very funny; but they kick them up with the sides or soles of their feet. The game must be a good deal more difficult than that played in England, I should fancy; but the Chinese seem fond of using their feet, and so, very likely, they are more expert with them than we are. You remember about the man rowing with his feet?"

"Oh yes—the man who rowed, and smoked, and managed a sail all at once; I remember," said Tom. "But, mamma, tell us something about Hongkong now. Did not you say it belongs to us?"

"Yes, it was ceded to England in 1841; and in the course of a very few years a most imposing town sprang up, which is called Victoria. Hongkong, I hope you remember, is an island just at the mouth of the river Choo-kiang."

"And what sort of people live there?" inquired Tom.

"Merchants principally," said Mrs. Foster. But though we have colonized the island, there is, of course, still a large Chinese population; and Mr. Wingrove Cook, who paid the island a visit some years ago, says that every English resident employs one of these natives as a kind of major-domo. The man hires all the servants, does all the marketing, pays all the bills, and generally manages the house. He says that, of course, he cheats unmercifully; but then he allows his master to be cheated by no one else."

"Well, I suppose, there is some advantage in that," said Tom. "It is better to be robbed by one thief than five hundred. But do these Chinese fellows learn English, or do all the English merchants have to learn Chinese?"

"Apparently a most curious kind of jargon has sprung up, and the first time Mr. Cook heard it spoken he thought his friend was talking Chinese. But it is only a most corrupt kind of English, and is, I believe, called commonly 'pigeon' English. Here is a specimen of it. Soon after Mr. Cook's arrival in the island, his Chinese servant woke him in the morning with the announcement, 'Missa Smith one small piecey cow child hab got.'"

"Whatever did he mean by that, mamma?" said Mabel.

"Just that Mrs. Smith had got a little girl. Here is another amusing specimen of Chinese English: 'Master,' said a Chinese lad, 'the dog hab five childs: three of them be bulls, and two cows.' Listen to another sentence, which I don't think any one of you will be able to understand: ' You see gentleman; you tawkee one piecey coolie, one piecey boy larnt pigeon, you savey, no number one foolo—you make see this gentleman—you make him home pigeon.'"

"What utter gibberish!" exclaimed several of the children. "Whatever did it all mean?"

"It is just the speech which Mr. Cook's friend made to his Chinese major-domo when he wanted to tell him to make comfortable arrangements for Mr. Cook during his stay in Hongkong. The meaning of the sentence was just this: 'You see this gentleman; you must engage for him a coolie and a boy—people who understand their business, you know, not stupid fellows. You will bring them to him, and then manage to get him a lodging, and furnish it.'"

"But what do they mean by calling it pigeon English?" inquired Grace.

"Well, 'pigeon,' I believe, is the nearest approach that a Chinese can make to the English word 'business,' and this jargon is used for business purposes."

"But why can't the people learn proper English while they are about it?" said Frank. "Two people must have to learn that stuff—the Chinese and the Englishman; and it must be nearly as difficult to the Englishman as to the Chinese. But is Hongkong a pleasant sort of place?"

"I suppose, as to that, there are differences of opinion, as there are about most matters. The climate appears to be a very trying one, the island being subject to very violent rains and, at the same time, exposed to a most scorching sun. I dare say it is not quite as unhealthy now as it was when first colonized, and that people know better how to live there than they did; but still it is not a place in which to do much hard work for any length of time, and people require an immense quantity of quinine there.

"One thing which makes Victoria such a very undesirable place to live in, as regards health, is the way in which the place is completely cut off from the refreshing south-west wind by a sugar-loaf-shaped mountain, called the Victoria Peak. The town, in fact, is, I suppose, just on the wrong side of this mountain."

"Is not there a place called the Happy Valley somewhere in Hongkong?" inquired Grace.

"Yes; and a very pretty spot it seems to be. It is a narrow gorge in the mountains, with a beautiful stream of clear, sparkling water running down it. It looks as if it would be a charming place to live in; but it is even more unhealthy, I fancy, than Victoria, and people have given it up as a place of residence. They have come to the conclusion that it is more fitted for a cemetery, and it is in the Happy Valley that the English people are buried."

"Is not there a Bishop of Victoria, mamma?" said Tom. "I am sure I remember hearing one speak at a missionary meeting once. It is a good while ago now; but I remember quite well one thing that he said—don't you, Grace? Don't you remember he said that the Chinese liked to be stout, because they considered people's brains to be where we put our dinners."

"Oh yes, I remember," said Grace; "but does the Bishop of Victoria look after the Chinese?"

"Well, I think all the Bishops of Victoria that there have ever been have done all they could to help the missionaries; and the present bishop was himself a most active and earnest missionary before he was made bishop; but the direct work of the Bishop of Victoria is to look after the English colonists rather than the heathen."

"Do you know, Mrs. Foster," said little Lucy, "I read in a book the other day that there were Christians in China in very early times; do you think that that is true?"

"I believe," replied Mrs. Foster, "that there is very good reason to believe that Christianity was preached in China in the first century, and that several churches were founded there. Of course, if that is the case, it was introduced into the country about the same time as Buddhism, and it is grievous to think how the one has flourished, while the other died out. But be that as it may, it appears quite certain, from a marble tablet that was discovered in 1625, and which was put up in 781, that the Nestorian Christians had missions in China in the sixth century, that their churches were very flourishing, and that they enjoyed the special patronage of a dynasty of emperors who reigned during the seventh and eighth centuries. Parts of the Bible were translated; and though, perhaps, the teaching may not have been altogether pure, it made great progress. However, in the ninth century a persecution arose, and the Christian priests were ordered to retire into private life. Still the churches continued to exist, until another fierce persecution arose about the middle of the sixteenth century. Then the poor Christians became utterly scattered, and their churches changed into heathen temples."

"And I suppose they gradually died out altogether?" said Mabel. "How very sad! It was something like the early British Church, wasn't it? But there are missions to the Nestorians now, aren't there?"

"Yes, because, like all those ancient eastern churches, they have become to a certain extent corrupt, and have also sunk into a very lukewarm, lifeless state."

"How dreadful it must have seemed to the poor Christians to have their churches turned into heathen temples!" said Grace.

"Yes," said Mrs. Foster, "unless they had first relapsed into heathenism. But it is, as you say, melancholy to think of heathen idols being set up in the house of God."

"And it seems so strange, too," said Tom, "that people who had once known about the true God could bring themselves to bow down before a hideous image."

"But the Chinese images aren't all hideous," said Frank, "are they, Mrs. Foster?"

"No, I do not think you can exactly call them that. Here is a picture of one, for instance, that is anything but hideous. On the contrary, it is a pretty, graceful figure. It is intended for a personification of Providence. Do you see the round plate in her hand, with an eye upon it?"

"Yes; what is it meant for?" said Tom.

"No doubt to represent foresight and carefulness," replied Mrs. Foster. "The eye gives the idea of continual watching. The figure is in a temple at a place called Tong-choo-foo. There is a monastery attached to it that was built some centuries ago. It was intended to accommodate twelve monks, but now is very much used as a kind of caravanserai, where travellers of rank are lodged as they pass through the country. It was here that the embassy which I have mentioned to you several times was accommodated, and they certainly seem to have been treated very well. Of course the ambassador had a great many people with him, so the monks gave up almost the whole of the building to him, and retired to another monastery somewhere in the neighbourhood, just one monk remaining behind to attend to the lamps in the temple."

"You see in the picture there is something burning," said Grace. "It does not look exactly like a lamp, though. But, mamma, I want to ask you about those rebels in China. I forget what they are called, but they are some people who made a great stir and commotion some time ago."

"The Taepings, do you mean?"

"Oh, yes, that was their name. Well, mamma, did not they knock down the idols a great deal?"

"Yes, they certainly did. An American missionary, the Rev. H. M. Parker, writing in 1861, says, 'I found some of the temples burnt down, others only torn down in part and defaced. In the interior I saw what struck me most. The images and idols were some thrown down and broken to pieces, some decapitated, and with the hands and feet cut off, others were only disfigured, having the noses cut off, the eyes bored out, or mouths cut from ear to ear; others again were turned upside down, or placed in the most ridiculous positions. In every conceivable way it was evidently their desire to show their own contempt for these objects of worship, and to excite that of their countrymen.' "

" But what sort of people are these Taepings, then?" inquired Frank. " Are they Christians?"

" No, they certainly cannot properly be called that," said Mrs. Foster, " though what they are it is not easy to say. At first, I suppose, the missionaries hoped a great deal from the movement, and the missionary from whom I quoted a few minutes ago, speaks a little further on of its ' having inflicted a death-blow on idolatry and superstition in many parts of the country,' and says that, on one occasion, on asking the people of some village which he visited, what gods they worshipped, they replied, ' that the rebels had destroyed their gods, and forbidden them to worship them, and now they had no gods, and would be glad to be taught the worship of some other.' "

" But how did it all begin?" inquired Tom, "and how long ago was it?"

" The outbreak began a good many years ago now, and the originator of it was a man called Hung-sew-tsuen. Somewhere about the year 1834, when he was about sixteen, a native Christian gave him a

FIGURE OF PROVIDENCE.

book called 'Good Words exhorting the Age.' The book contained a number of short sermons on different passages of Scripture and the general principles of religion, and was bound in four pretty large volumes. Whether Hung-sew-tsuen received the whole of the book, or only a part, is not known, but, at any rate, he read it, and certain passages gained a firm hold of his mind, particularly 'that men ought truly to believe in God, in Jesus, obey the Ten Commandments, and not worship devils.' A short time after this he had a very bad illness, and was, I suppose, extremely delirious; but he imagined that he had in spirit been taken up into heaven, and there had had revelations of the true doctrine. He got up from his sick bed firmly persuaded that he was commissioned to do an important work. He immediately began to travel about, distributing books written by himself, and talking to all who would listen, and persuaded a great many to join themselves to him. About the year 1846 or 1847 he visited Canton, and applied to the Rev. T. J. Roberts, an American missionary, for instruction in the Christian religion. He remained with him about two months, and wanted to be baptized. But Mr. Roberts was not fully satisfied with regard to his fitness. After he left Canton he began teaching again, until some of the Chinese authorities interfered, and two of his adherents were put to death. He and his followers now combined for self-defence, and the movement rapidly assumed a political character. At one time it seemed likely that the reigning dynasty would be overturned, and some imagined that Hung-sew-tsuen would prove a second Mahomet. But it did not prove so. Gradually the movement subsided."

"But was there much bloodshed, mamma?" said Grace.

"Well, I suppose it is always difficult to be certain whether the information one gains is correct, but by some it is estimated that the population of China is about half what it was before the rebellion broke out."

"I should hope that is an exaggeration," said Mabel. "That seems rather a fearful account. But did they take any of the large cities?"

"Yes, Hang-chow and Ningpo were both sacked. Hung-sew-tsuen apparently considered himself specially commissioned by Heaven to conquer and subdue the 'fiends,' by which he evidently meant the Manchow Tartars."

"But what did he believe, mamma? Did he believe in the Lord Jesus Christ at all?"

"Yes, he did; but, as far as I can make out, he looked upon Him as an earthly rather than a heavenly Saviour—a Saviour in the sense in which Joshua was a Saviour, rather than a Saviour from sin. He was continually called 'the celestial king;' and in one document which he put into the hands of Mr. Roberts, he says that he is the Son of God in exactly the same way as the Lord Jesus Christ was."

"How very horrible!" exclaimed Mabel. "But did not the missionaries at one time think that the Taepings might do a great deal of good?"

"Yes, they did. They looked upon them as men who were gradually groping their way out of the darkness. But then you must not forget that these blasphemous pretensions were not put forth at first. And a great deal of their teaching was very good. They distinctly taught that there is but one God, 'one heavenly Father and supreme Lord, who is omniscient, omnipotent, and omnipresent; the supreme over all;' they recognized the Ten Commandments as the rule of life, and though it certainly was far from occupying the place which it ought to have done in their teaching, they did acknowledge the Saviour's work of redemption.

"Of course the missionaries very much hoped that

the Taepings would encourage their preaching, and with one of the leaders of the rebellion, called the Kan-wang, they had many interviews. But they were grievously disappointed to find that he always thought it was the wrong time. He was always very cordial to them, but they soon found that his excuses for declining to co-operate with them in the great work of teaching the pure gospel to the people were mere excuses. It was the gospel itself that he did not like.

"And yet, from the resemblance between the gospel and the teaching of the Taepings, the missionaries were, during the time of the disturbances, not unfrequently confounded with the Taepings, and, therefore, exposed to considerable danger from the Imperialist party. The present Bishop of Victoria—who was at that time a missionary in the country—gives an account of his having been attacked, seized, and taken before a mandarin, while teaching and distributing books, the soldier who conducted him continually whispering in his ear, 'You are no foreigner,' meaning, no doubt, that he was one of the Taeping rebels."

"And did the mandarin do anything to him?" inquired Grace.

"No; on the contrary, the mandarin listened very

calmly to all that Mr. Burdon had to say, accepted some books, and granted permission for the distribution of these books to go on."

"Well, the disturbance did not do him much harm, after all," said Tom.

"Not as it turned out, but still it showed how apt the poor people were to confound the missionaries and the rebels. The mandarin, too, was one of very high rank. He might not have found it so easy to quiet the disturbance, had he been a less distinguished man himself."

"I suppose Mr. Burdon judged of his rank by his button, did he not?" said Frank.

"No doubt, but also from the manner in which the people all fell on their knees before him. The people round wanted to make Mr. Burdon do the same, but apparently he did not see it, and his companion, Mr. Taylor, says that his knees stiffened involuntarily."

"Is not there some kind of act of worship which the Emperor demands from those who enter his presence?" inquired Mabel.

"Yes, but I think the English have always been excused from performing it. It was demanded of the ambassador whom I have so many times mentioned to you; but, when he objected, he was informed that the Emperor would be satisfied with the same token of respect that he would offer to his own monarch. Altogether, the Emperor seems to have behaved very politely, both to the ambassador and his

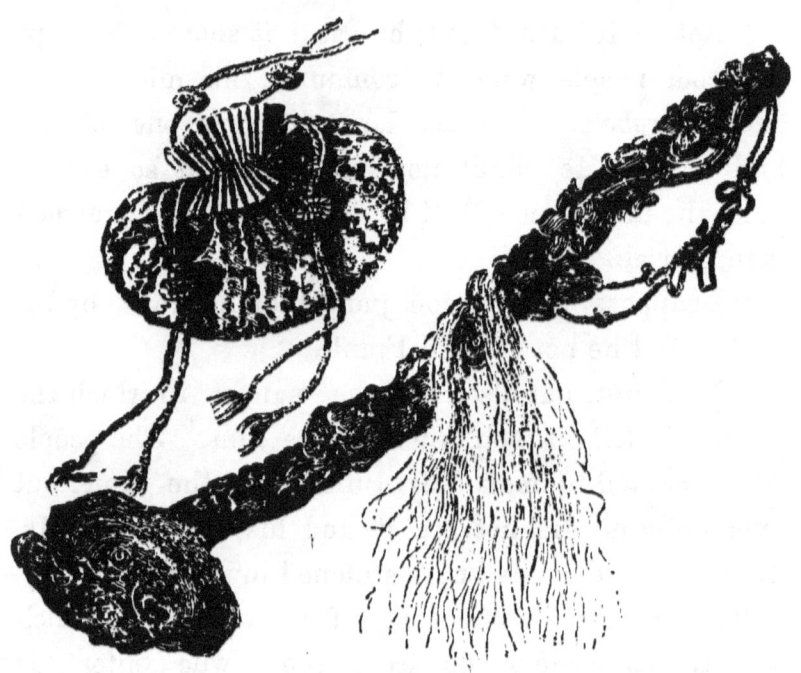

PURSE AND SCEPTRE.

train. Here is the picture of a purse which he presented to the ambassador's page, a lad of thirteen."

"And what did he give it him for?" inquired Tom.

"Just in order to show the boy that he was pleased to find that he had taken the trouble to learn some Chinese. The mandarins always afterwards took a great deal of notice of the fortunate boy, for this purse had been used by his Imperial Majesty, and such a gift was considered a special honour."

"But what is that other thing in the picture? It is a most curious looking article. It seems to be all carved."

"It is a sceptre. Just such an one also as the Emperor often gives as a present. But I think we must not talk any more to-day. It is past our proper time for stopping, and we shall be accused of unpunctuality if you young people are late home."

CHAPTER XI.

SOLDIERS.

"I SUPPOSE this will be our last working party for a little while, won't it, mamma?" said Mabel, at the next meeting.

"Yes; holidays are beginning. There is hay to be made; excursions to be taken; visits to the seaside to be paid; and all sorts of fun to be had; so it will be better, no doubt, to postpone our next gathering until October, when you will all set to work with fresh vigour."

"We have got through a good deal of work this year," said Grace; "and the boys things will be something so fresh and new that they are sure to sell well. I expect we shall find that the work will produce a good deal more than it has ever yet done."

"Well, then we must find the Chinese boy that we talked about," said Mrs. Foster. "I dare say we shall not have much trouble to do so."

"Won't you tell us something about the Chinese

CHINESE SOLDIERS DRAWN OUT TO SALUTE THE ENGLISH AMBASSADOR.

soldiers to-day, mamma?" said Tom. "You were talking about the Taeping rebellion last time, and about the fights between the rebels and the Imperialists, and I want to know what the soldiers look like, how they are dressed, and whether they fight well, and all that sort of thing."

"I believe the Tartars make far better soldiers than the native Chinese, and the principal officers of confidence are generally of that race. They are generally finer and bigger men. Here is a picture of a body of soldiers drawn up to salute the Embassy as it went by.

"That is the same Embassy that you have told us about before, I suppose?" said Grace.

"Yes," replied Mrs. Foster. "I believe in every large city in China a considerable body of soldiers are kept, and when the barges that contained the ambassador and his train came near the walls of any of these, about three hundred soldiers were at once drawn up along the shores of the river or canal, as it might happen to be. An officers' tent was pitched, the military band began to play, and a salute was fired."

"Oh yes, look," said Tom, "the gunner has just fired the cannon. But how oddly the thing seems placed, straight up in the air, and what a little thing it looks, too!"

"It is just a small petard. Three was the number that were fired at each place, and that was the way that they were placed. They were fired off just as the barge which contained the ambassador himself passed the officers' tent.

"I wish the soldiers were drawn a little bigger," said Frank, "I can't see how they are dressed. They only look very fat, and as if they had got a great many clothes on."

"I think I can tell you a little about their dress," said Mrs. Foster, "though I cannot be sure that my description will be altogether correct now, for it is taken from a very old book. Still, as you see the Chinese are not given to change, probably not many alterations have been made. It is the dress of the cavalry. First of all there is a helmet made of iron, and in shape like a funnel turned wrong side upwards. At the top there is something like a little spear, and this is surmounted by a red tassel. The neck is protected by a piece of cloth stuffed, quilted, and studded with iron, which hangs forward round the face. Then, below this, there are two other garments, both also quilted, and studded with iron. The lower one reaches a little below the calves, and the upper one comes just beyond the waist. The dress of the officers is of the same kind, only more magnificent. Their helmets are polished and ornamented with gold, and the crest is higher than that of the common men. The under and upper garments, too, are made of purple or blue silk, and studded with gold instead of iron.

"What a disagreeable sort of dress it must be!" said Tom. "It must be as heavy as armour, and yet can't be of the same use. But don't the soldiers have anything on their feet?"

"Yes; but I don't think you would ever guess what. Black satin boots with paper soles!"

"What an idea!" exclaimed Frank. "Why, I should think they must want a new pair every week."

"Well, I should think so too," replied Mrs. Foster. "I really can't tell you how they manage. But now I will tell you about another dress which some of the soldiers wear. It is made of yellow cloth with dark brown stripes, and fits close to the shape. It is called the tiger dress, and the cap, which nearly covers the face, is made to resemble as closely as possible the head of a tiger."

"What horrible frights the soldiers who are dressed like that must look!" said Mabel.

"Yes," said Mrs. Foster. "I believe the idea is to make them look as terrific as possible, and, in order to add to their awful appearance, the shields that they carry—made of bamboo—are hideously painted, to represent dragons' or tigers' heads."

"And what sort of weapons do they use?" said Tom.

"Those soldiers only carry swords. But the cavalry are, or at any rate used to be, armed with bows. These bows are made of an elastic wood, strengthened by horns, which are connected in the centre by their roots. The string is made of silk threads."

"How fond the Chinese seem to be of silk, don't they?" said Grace. "I suppose it is because they have such a quantity of it in the country."

"No doubt," replied Mrs. Foster. "And then, you know that silk is so strong that I dare say it makes very good bow-strings. The Chinese arrows are said to be perfectly well turned and feathered, and are armed at the points with a shank and spear of steel. Both Tartars and Chinese pride themselves on their skill in the use of the bow. I will try and describe to you how they shoot with it. The right thumb of the archer is furnished with an agate ring, and the string of the bow is placed behind this ring. The bow is held in an oblique position, and the thumb bent by pressing the middle joint of the forefinger with it. The left arm is then extended until it is quite straight, and the right arm drawn back until it passes the right ear. The forefinger is then suddenly withdrawn from the thumb, which instantly forces the string from the agate ring, and discharges the arrow with considerable force."

"But I suppose the Chinese have found out by this time that gunpowder can be used for fighting purposes. Surely they have their guns?" said Grace.

"Certainly," replied Mrs. Foster. "They could scarcely have fought as they have done with European nations without finding out that it is useless to contend against them with other weapons. In the account of the war which England had with China in 1857 and 1858, Mr. Wingrove Cook, who was special correspondent for the *Times*, made frequent mention of the Chinese forts and guns. The Bogue forts, for instance, somewhere not very far from Canton, he describes as being very formidable. There are four large batteries, each having embrasures for a hundred monstrous guns. He says, too, that the

Chinese complained that the English did not fight fairly when they took these forts. They said that, instead of going boldly at them, like brave men, they just sent a few small ships to be fired at, and then, while the gunners were busy, a few soldiers leapt over a wall in the rear, and drove the gunners out."

"Well, and why shouldn't they?" said Tom. "I suppose they thought the English ought to have sent them a full description of the way in which they meant to attack. A fine idea, indeed!"

"Very," said Mrs. Foster. "One day, apparently, some one asked one of these gunners why he ran away from a storming party. 'No can,' he replied; 'two piecey man no can stand all same place. S'pose you must come in, I go out.'"

"Is the Chinese army a large one?" inquired Frank. "I should think it must require an immense number of men to defend such an enormous country."

"Yes," replied Mrs. Foster, "and China has not the advantage of being an island, like our nice little kingdom. But I really cannot tell you the exact number of the Chinese forces. Bodies of military, as I told you, are stationed in every large town, and besides that there are numbers of military posts throughout the country. They are generally placed at the entrances of difficult passes, or on hills that are hard to climb, or at the narrow parts of rivers. These posts, in ordinary times, have just a few men stationed in them, but in times of war no doubt they are used as places of rendezvous for all the troops of the neighbourhood."

"What sort of places are they?" inquired Frank.

"They are generally square towers, and vary very much in point of size. Sometimes they are about forty feet square, and as many feet high, while some are as small as four feet square, and six feet high."

"What absurd little places those must be!" said Tom. "I should not think there are many of them."

"No, I believe there are not. The bigger ones are more common. These towers are generally made quite solid, and are ascended by a staircase on the outside. At the top of the tower there is generally a little building, and on one end of this there is a flagstaff, on which a yellow standard is hoisted. Stay, I believe I have a picture of one of these forts in my portfolio. Run and fetch it, Grace. I had almost forgotten it, and that would have been a pity, after taking special care of it for you. I met with it some little time ago now."

Grace soon brought the portfolio, and gave it to her mother.

"This is the picture," said Mrs. Foster, as she handed it round the table. "Besides showing you a little what the Chinese forts are like, if you look closely you will see that there are some of the tiger-dressed soldiers in the corner."

"Oh yes, don't you see, Mabel?" said Tom, who was leaning over his sister's shoulder. "How queer they do look! and what is that place at the right side of the tower? It looks as if it had got some guns stuck in it."

"That is what it is meant for, I think," said Mrs. Foster. "There is generally a red stand for arms somewhere close by one of these towers, where a few muskets and spears are displayed."

"There certainly cannot be many men kept at such a place as this," said Tom. "How many are there generally, mamma?"

"The number, no doubt, varies according to the size of the place. Sometimes, I believe, there are not more than six men, and at some of the posts as many as fifteen may be seen."

Whenever any person of importance passes one of the posts, the men are all drawn out, dressed in their

A MILITARY POST.

best military attire, and then, when he is gone by, they take their things off again, and fold them up carefully."

"But how can they get dressed in time?" inquired Mabel. "How can they know beforehand that any one is coming?"

"A soldier is stationed on the top of the tower, just as you see in the picture; and he gives the signal by striking on an instrument called a loo."

Mrs. Foster paused for a moment, and Tom said, " I suppose the Chinese consider their country all splendid, since they think it so much better than any other; but is there any part that they admire more than the rest?"

"Well, I believe it is a common saying among them," replied his mother, "that heaven is above them, but on the earth they have Sou-chou-foo. It is a town on the grand canal, not far from Shanghai, and even by travellers it is called 'the paradise of China,' so I suppose it is very beautiful. Before its desolation by the Taepings, it was an exceedingly prosperous city. In size and riches it is said to have surpassed Nankin, the city proper occupying an area of ten miles. It had also four immense suburbs, and all the country in the neighbourhood was highly cultivated. Its people, too, were so noted for their good looks that there was a national proverb, 'To be happy on earth one must be born in Sou-chou, live in Canton, and die at Lian-chan,' for in the first there are the handsomest people, in the second the richest luxuries, and in the third the best coffins. I should hope that by this time it may in some measure have recovered its prosperity, but its condition after it had been sacked by the rebels is described as most heartrending.

When first threatened, the whole of the suburban buildings were, merely as a defensive measure, destroyed, but it was of no avail. The Taepings soon made themselves masters of the place. The Imperialists saw that all resistance was useless, and yielded almost without a struggle, the general putting an end to himself in his despair. The place was visited shortly after the sack by the present Bishop of Victoria, who was a simple missionary; and from his account it appears that the streets were deserted, many of the houses ruined, household furniture lay strewn about, while corpses everywhere filled the air with the taint of death. This of course was a good while ago, and, as I said, I should hope the place has, to a certain extent at any rate, got over the calamity. The natural resources are very great. There is a beautiful lake in the neighbourhood which furnishes an abundant supply of fish, and there are also enormous forests of mulberry trees."

"I suppose it had great silk manufactories then?" said Grace.

"Yes, before it was taken by the Taepings, they were a great source of wealth. It had also manufactories of cotton fabrics and works in iron, ivory, wood, horn, glass, lacquered ware, and paper.

"Of course the deep distress in which the natives of the town were after the rebels took it, presented a favourable opportunity for the missionaries to step in with the offer of the gospel, but I cannot find out that much has yet been done there. Missionary societies never are able to do all they might, just for want of money and men."

"But there are a great many more missionaries in China now than there used to be a few years ago, are there not?" said Mabel.

"Certainly, my dear," said Mrs. Foster. "Since the country has been open, every society at work there has of course striven to do more, and the number of missionaries employed, for instance, by the Church Missionary Society, has steadily increased. They have now missionaries stationed in nine of the eighteen provinces of China.

"Before we stop, I want to tell you a little about the early life of a Chinese clergyman, who was ordained in 1868. His name was Wong Kin Taik. Wong is his surname, so we will call him Wong. Well, Mr. Wong was a young landscape painter, and lived in Fuh-chau. He had an intimate friend named Hu-tong-mi, who had become a convert to Christianity through the preaching of some of the American missionaries. Having found peace and happiness himself, Hu-tong-mi, like a true friend, was anxious that Wong should become a sharer of the same. He prayed much for him, and talked a great deal to him, and it was soon evident that his efforts were not thrown away. Wong began earnestly to study the Scriptures, and to attend the meetings of the missionaries.

"For a time all went on peaceably, but soon some one warned his mother, who was a widow, and most tenderly attached to her son, that he was running into danger, and she had better look after him. She anxiously inquired what was the matter, and was horrified when she heard that there was any danger of her son becoming a Christian. On the first opportunity she questioned him about it. He answered her very humbly and modestly, saying that he was young, and did not understand all that was said, but that what the foreign teachers said seemed to him very reasonable. Finding that she could not persuade him to abstain from attending the meetings of the missionaries, she forbade him to stir out of the house. 'Henceforth,' she said, 'you must not cross the threshold of my door to go abroad. Stay here and work, and when you have prepared the pictures I will attend to selling them.'

"The young man meekly submitted, and for a good while the old lady kept him a close prisoner to the house, narrowly watching him to see that he did not make his escape."

"But how could he bear it?" said Tom. "It was not as if he were a little child, or even a boy. I should never have thought that a young man would have submitted to such a thing."

"Few young Englishmen would, I expect; and few English mothers would have attempted it." But you must not forget the extreme reverence which all Chinamen feel for their parents. A mother's curse is about the greatest calamity that can befall any one. Still, though Wong submitted, the restraint was a bitter trial to him, and, of course, his mother did not let him. She was continually trying to shake his determination to become a Christian, weeping, imploring, and scolding by turns.

"In his distress poor Wong sought comfort, frequently retiring to his own room to pour out his griefs before God. But his mother found this out, for, in his earnestness, Wong not unfrequently prayed aloud, and as she listened she would often hear the name of Jesus. This was more than she could bear. She peremptorily ordered her son to cease praying. But this he felt he could not yield. 'Mother,' he said, 'hitherto I have obeyed all your commands, but now, when you tell me to cease praying to God, I dare not obey you.' 'But the noise disturbs me,' said the old lady, 'I cannot stay in the house with you.' 'Mother,' replied Wong, 'I did not know that I prayed so loud; henceforth I will pray in a whisper, so that you need not be disturbed.' 'You shall never pray again in my house,' sternly replied the mother; 'if you continue to pray you must leave the house.' 'Mother,' said poor Wong, 'I cannot cease to pray.'"

"And did she really turn him out?" inquired Grace. "She surely could not have the heart to do so."

"Yes," replied Mrs. Foster, "she did; and, more than that, she disowned him as her child, forbade him ever to re-enter her door, and to take any part in her funeral obsequies when she should die."

"And what did the poor fellow do?" asked Mabel.

"He went to live with his friend Hu, and some months passed peacefully away. He was now, of course, able to attend the services again, and to hold intercourse with the other Christians. He studied his Bible continually, and became more and more firmly established in the Christian faith.

"But one day he came to Dr. Mackay, the missionary, in great alarm and perplexity. His mother, he said, had sent for him. Should he go? He heard that his heathen relatives wanted to get him into their power that they might either beat or kill him.

"Dr. Mackay, as you may imagine, was very much puzzled as to what advice he ought to give. 'Oh! how profoundly,' he says, 'I felt the need of heavenly wisdom to direct me.' After weighing the matter, he advised him to go and maintain his integrity at all hazards.

"For a few minutes a hard struggle evidently went on within poor Wong; but at length he said, 'I will go, pray for me.'

"And he went. You can fancy the anxiety with which Dr. Mackay awaited the result, and what earnest petitions he sent up on his behalf.

"The next day Wong returned with a most joyful countenance, and a strange tale he had to tell. His mother had met him with the question, which, she said, she put for the last time, whether he would abandon his purpose of becoming a Christian. 'Mother,' Wong replied, 'I have forsaken the evil, and am following the good. How can I now abandon the good, and turn to the evil?' 'You are fully determined, then,' said his mother, 'to become a Christian?' Poor Wong lifted his heart to God, and prayed for strength to give a faithful answer, and replied, 'I am determined.'

"Of course he expected at once to receive his mother's most bitter malediction; but, to his utter surprise, after looking at him steadily for a few minutes, she said, 'If I cannot change your determination, I shall change mine. I shall not oppose you any further. You are at liberty to become a Christian, and I wish you to live with me as formerly.'"

"How wonderful!" exclaimed Grace. "And how delighted poor Wong must have been! He must have felt almost as Abraham did when God called to him out of heaven, and said, 'Lay not thine hand upon the lad.' He had given up his mother for God, and then God suddenly gave her back to him again. Did she ever become a Christian, mamma? I should almost think she must have."

"I should think so too, Grace," replied Mrs. Foster; "but I can find no account of her conversion. Whether God saw fit to answer her son's prayers on her behalf, therefore, I cannot tell; but it is not so long ago since what I have been telling you happened, and she may still be alive. Wong himself was baptized in 1857, and for two years worked as a kind of Evangelist, under the American Episcopal Methodist Mission. After a time he joined our Church Missionary Society, and, having laboured for a good while as Catechist, was at length ordained by the Bishop of Victoria."

www.ingramcontent.com/pod-product-compliance
Lightning Source LLC
Chambersburg PA
CBHW021409230426
43666CB00006B/692